Personal Finance Strategies for a Secure Retirement

Simple Strategies to Enjoy a Secure Retirement

By: Andy LaPointe

Disclaimer:

The information in this course is for educational purposes only. The information is not financial, trading or tax advice or recommendations. The publisher and author bear no responsibility or control over the actions of those who take this course. Investing involve a very high degree of risk. Past results are not indicative of future returns.

The indicators and strategies mentioned in this course are for educational purposes only and should not be construed as investment advice. The publisher and author does not warrant its completeness or accuracy or warrant any results from the use of the information.

The reader uses the information in this course at their own risk and it is their sole responsibility. The reader needs to evaluate the accuracy, completeness and usefulness of the information.

The reader isn't guaranteed of any profit, making money and may even loss all of their money. The readers trading strategies may be consistent or inconsistent with the information provided.

Introduction:

Written by a retired Registered Investment Advisor and mutual fund wholesaler, you'll learn proven personal strategies to enjoy a secure retirement in your golden years. The purpose of this book is to provide targeted financial insight and advice to those currently in retirement or approaching retirement.

The information in this book is meant to provide you with an outline and guidance for every area of retirement. You'll learn insight the following areas:

- Strategies to build a diversified portfolio
- How to avoid scams and fraud
- Strategies to improve your estate plan
- What types of insurance to consider during ret
- What to consider when gifting assets
- And much more…

This format of this book is to provide areas to consider and provide little-known strategies used by high net-worth individuals for a secure retirement future.

About the Author: Mr. LaPointe spent 15 years in the corporate world as a Registered Investment Advisor (RIA) and mutual fund wholesaler. He worked with countless high net worth families, business owners, professional football players to create a secure retirement.

Contents

Disclaimer: 0

Introduction: 2

Personal Finance Strategies for a Secure Retirement 5

    4 Critical Steps to Retiring When You Want 5

    Top 5 Costs That Retirees Often Fail to Foresee 7

    Top 5 Reasons Why You Might Like an Index Fund if You're Retired 9

    Top Guilty Pleasures That Come with Hidden Expenses 11

    Retire Sooner with These Strategies 13

    Smart Strategies for Investing During Retirement 15

    Taking Responsibility for Your Financial Situation 17

    Rich and Staying That Way: 5 Strategies for Keeping Your Wealth 19

    Avoid These Mistakes When Saving for Retirement 25

    Do You Struggle with Compulsive Spending? 27

    How to Live Successfully Without a Car 30

    How to Prepare for Financial Challenges 32

    Preparing for Early Retirement: Tax Implications of Your Money-Making Hobby 34

Financial Strategies Regarding Divorce in Retirement 36

    Discover How to Survive a Divorce with Your Finances Intact 36

    You'll Be Okay: Financially Adjusting to Divorce 38

    How to Eliminate Money Arguments in Your Marriage 40

    Habits of Financially Successful Singles 43

Vacation Tips 45

    7 Tips to Save Money on Your Next Vacation 45

    What If... You Had a Vacation with No Bills? 47

Strategies to Reduce Expenses in Retirement 49

    9 Ways to Cut Prescription Costs 49

    5 Costly Surprises of Retirement 51

    10 Things That Are Better to Buy Used 53

    Which State Offers You The Best Tax Advantages for Your Retirement? 55

    Easy Ways to Cut Retirement Expenses 57

Estate Planning Strategies 59

    Beware of These Top 7 Estate Planning Mistakes 59

- Give Living Inheritances to Your Kids with Tax-Free Techniques 61
- Top Reasons to Revise Your Will 63

Insurance Strategies 65
- Renter's Insurance and Retirees 65
- 6 Unusual Insurance Policies You Might Want to Consider 67
- Could You Benefit from Umbrella Liability Insurance? 69
- Don't Let Insurance Fraud Devastate Your Financial Plans 71
- Learn Annuity Pay-out Choices to Meet Your Retirement Needs 74

Real Estate Owner Ship 76
- Relying on Home Equity for Retirement Could Spell Disaster 76
- Renter's Insurance and Retirees 78
- Beware of These 5 Common Foreclosure Scams 80
- 5 Great Retirement Locations for the Budget-Minded 82
- Top Reasons to Revise Your Will 84
- The Top 6 Home Improvements with the Best Return 86

Personal Finance Strategies for a Secure Retirement

4 Critical Steps to Retiring When You Want

Are you on track with being able to retire when you want to? It's so easy to procrastinate about investing money for your retirement – especially if you're a long way away from your retirement date. But starting early makes it so much easier to meet your retirement goals.

How much do want to save? A million dollars? Keep in mind that no one reached age 65 and complained that they saved too much! Many folks believe that you have to have a significant income to save a million dollars, but nothing could be further from the truth.

Saving steadily and starting as soon as possible can make it possible for anyone to retire a millionaire.

Follow these steps to get yourself quickly on track:

1. **Take an assessment.** Where are you right now financially? How much have you saved so far? What is your current income? What are you current expenses? How much are you currently saving? What changes can you make right now that will make the biggest difference? Do you need the advice of an expert?

    - Your best plans for moving forward toward your goals begin with an accurate idea of where you are right now. Ascertain your progress at least every year.

2. **Start saving today.** Most of us would rather buy a new TV today than save for a retirement that might not happen for 30 years. If you can enroll in a program that has automatic deductions, like a company 401(k) plan or an automatic-deduction brokerage account, saving can be a lot easier.

    - How you save isn't nearly as important as the saving itself. Just start immediately! Even a relatively small amount can really add up over the years.

3. **Make a plan.** Make an honest evaluation of how much money you'll most likely need to retire and live comfortably for the remainder of your life. Then take a look at how much you need to save between now and then to make it happen. There are many financial planning calculators available online to help with your planning.

    - Imagine how much better your retirement savings would be right now if you had developed a plan and implemented it 10 years ago. Don't wait another day. Today is the day.

    - *The Power of Compounding.* In making your plan, remember the tremendous power of compounding! At 10% interest, an 18 year old only needs to save $20 a week to amass a million dollars by age 65. A 30 year old: $67 a week. A 40 year old: $188 a week. The earlier you start, the less painful the saving process will be.

    - Include other money that goes into your plan as well. For example, if your employer matches 100% of your retirement plan contributions, you only need to put in half the required amount. If you'll have other income in retirement, like rental or social security income or money from a business or trust, include those in your figures.

4. **Consider These 3 Factors.** *The 3 most important factors to your success are the rate of return, the amount of money being saved, and time.* So invest well, invest a lot, and invest as soon as you can. Maximizing these three factors to the best of your ability is really the key to retiring in style and as soon as possible.

You don't have to be wealthy to retire a millionaire if you live below your means, save, and invest. The most important thing is to start saving immediately.

Even with a lower middle-class income, you can easily become a millionaire by maximizing the rate of return, amount saved, and time. Get aggressive with your savings plan and you'll retire in style.

Top 5 Costs That Retirees Often Fail to Foresee

Many folks nearing retirement fail to fully appreciate just how expensive retirement can be. *Have you really sat down and considered the expenses you're likely to face in retirement?*

Whether your vision of retirement includes traveling the world in first-class or staying at home with the grandkids, there are likely to be expenses that you either failed to consider or drastically underestimated.

It's important to accurately estimate your expenses in order to fully enjoy your retirement.

Consider these costs:

1. **Recreation.** One error many retirees make is assuming their recreational or entertainment expenses will stay the same. In most cases, they will not. Consider that while you're working, work takes up the largest part of your day. It likely accounts for around 10 hours of your day if you include driving and getting ready for work.

   - You'll probably want to spend all of that newfound freedom doing something other than watching TV. Traveling, going out to eat, playing golf, and shopping cost a lot more than going to work. *Consider that you're replacing 10 hours of income-producing activity with activities that likely cost money.*

2. **Cable, internet, utilities, property taxes, and other basic living expenses.** Hopefully, you'll have successfully eliminated your housing expense by paying off your mortgage. But you'll still have to pay property taxes, and they're unlikely to decrease over time. The same goes for the other monthly expenses you likely incur.

   - In the future, your utility bills are almost certainly going to increase. It's important to take this factor into consideration when making your retirement plans.

   - The cost of food will also likely increase over time.

   - The same goes for most, if not all, types of insurance.

3. **Health care expenses.** Ultimately, this is the biggest expense for many retirees. ***The average total cost of medical care right now for a 65-year old couple is over $270,000.*** Seventy percent of the population over the age of 65 will require long-term care at some point. Depending on the option you choose, this can be very expensive.

   - Assisted living facilities average approximately $3,500 per month.
   - A private nursing home is approximately $8,000 per month.
   - In-home care is roughly $50 hour for a certified home health aide.

4. **Miscellaneous expenses.** You never know what new interests you might develop. Maybe golf never sounded interesting, but you developed friendships with those that love to play. Perhaps you'll develop a love of art and would like to start collecting.

   - ***Assume you'll find new hobbies and interests and try to plan accordingly.***

5. **Unexpected expenses.** A major automobile repair just after the warranty expired or one of the children needing money can throw a wrench in your finances. Having an emergency fund is a good idea, regardless of your stage in life.

It can be challenging to plan for retirement. Both your income and your expenses are changing. ***While it's not possible to foresee every expense, many expenses can be anticipated.*** You have more free time. You're going to want to fill that time with interesting and meaningful activities.

Begin planning for your retirement today. Carefully consider the lifestyle you'd like to live and the expenses necessary to support that lifestyle.

Top 5 Reasons Why You Might Like an Index Fund if You're Retired

Index funds are a form of passive investing. They're passive for the investor and the fund manager. **Many people believe they want actively managed investments, but the data shows that index funds actually do better when adjusted for risk.**

Passive investments aren't as exciting as active investments. We all like to think our investing expertise has value, but for most of us, that simply isn't true. Very few mutual funds, headed by the best money managers in the world, can outperform an index fund when the active fund's fees are included in the equation. It's not easy to pick stocks that outperform the market.

Index funds are a great way for any investor to get good returns while mitigating risks. Passive investments like index funds have other characteristics that become more relevant as the investor gets older.

These are the reasons that retirees should consider investing in index funds:

1. **Passive investments simply require less time to monitor and manage.** You can spend your retirement on things that are more enjoyable.

   - Researching funds and stocks might have been something you were willing to do back in the day, but do you really want to do that now? Of course, this assumes that you were good at finding great investments in the first place.

   - Most of us would rather spend our retirement traveling, playing golf, going out to lunch, or spending time with family.

2. **The downs are less emotionally stressful.** While it's not enjoyable to watch any type of portfolio lose value, an index fund is much more likely to recover than an individual stock. The economy rarely shrinks. It generally grows, though at differing rates.

   - **Even if your index fund loses value, it is highly likely to come back in a timely fashion.**

   - Imagine spending your retirement years worrying about recovering from the dramatic downslide of a specific stock. This is the last thing most of us want.

3. **Taxes are less complicated.** Active portfolios involve a lot of buying and selling. Each sale has a tax implication of some sort. Your typical tax preparer isn't equipped to deal with a lot of these transactions.

   - A lot of active trading will likely require you to hire a CPA, and those folks bill by the hour.

4. **Index funds are an easy way to invest internationally.** With an index fund, you're basically investing in an economy. ***Somewhere in the world, there is an economy that's thriving.*** There are one or more index funds available for each of the major economies of the world.

5. **What happens when you die?** Can your spouse or children deal with the day trading mess that you leave behind? If you've been tweaking your investments for the last 20 years, can someone with little knowledge come in and harvest those gains properly?

    - It's still an issue with index funds, but the level of complexity is much smaller.

    - There is also a period of time shortly following your death where your portfolio will likely be unmanaged. If you're day trading, there's no one to make your trades unless someone else has access to your accounts. What could happen to your investments if they aren't managed for a few weeks?

Consider adding one or more index funds to your portfolio. ***Spend your retirement doing enjoyable things*** rather than slaving over your investments and struggling to complete your tax return.

Top Guilty Pleasures That Come with Hidden Expenses

Although advertising has led you to believe that businesses offering products and services exist to make your life better, ***they really exist to make money!*** The main reason for a business venture is to make a profit.

Keep this thought at the top of your mind when you consider "amazing" offers. Even though they seem to be offering you the best deal ever, ***it's your responsibility to ensure you're not being lured into hidden financial obligations.***

Hidden expenses can mean the difference between your financial wellness and growing debt.

Take a look at some of the top guilty pleasures below. If you think back, you'll probably remember being caught once or twice in similar situations!

Avoid these "deals" so you aren't faced with hidden expenses down the road:

1. **Financing a brand new car.** Just flipping through channels on cable will open your eyes to the awesome offers being extended by automobile manufacturers. "Zero down payments," "No interest for two years," and "Your job is your credit" are some of the offers to convince consumers like you to own the new car of your dreams.

    - In many cases, there will be a destination charge applied to your final price. This represents the cost for delivering a car to a dealer. It is paid for by the dealer and then passed along to you as a portion of the sales price.

    - Auto detailing and adding fluids are some of the activities in what is known as dealer preparation, but don't think these services are free! ***It's always a good idea to ask your retailer what their preparation fees are before you sign.***

    - ***What can really catch you off guard is sales tax.*** Depending on the state you live in, you could end up paying as much as eight percent in sales tax, which would add a huge chunk to your final total!

2. **Using your credit card for family vacations.** It's a great feeling to be able to take your family on vacation and treat them to a special trip, isn't it? ***But what are you really signing up for when you pay for the trip with your credit card?***

   - Do you have enough income to pay for the vacation in full the next month when the statement is generated? Or will you end up being in arrears for months because you couldn't resist that 14-day Mediterranean cruise?

   - Paying off your vacation over time costs a huge chunk of money in interest charges. Plus, you'll be stuck with higher credit card payments for months, causing an extra drain on your income.

   - ***A rule of thumb is to only use your credit card for purchases that you can comfortably make with cash.***

3. **Applying for "free" member rewards cards.** Everywhere you turn, there's a business offering you a "free" member rewards card. However, ***promises of no obligations when you sign up often lead to obligations later down the road.***

   - Whether it's a department store or your family's favorite amusement park, it's likely that you'll have to spend a minimum amount in order to benefit from their rewards program.

   - Oftentimes, the rewards pale in comparison to the amount of money you actually spend to get them!

So, the next time you see a tempting offer, ***ask yourself, "What's in it for them?"*** The answer to that question will surely clue you in to what hidden expenses you might expect down the road.

Retire Sooner with These Strategies

Do you find yourself feeling like you won't ever have enough money to stop working? If so, it's time to perk up.

Use these strategies to retire sooner than you ever dreamed of:

1. **Identify activities that bring you joy and then create an income stream doing them.** When you retire, you'll have more free time to fill up. Why not do it engaging in activities you love and earning some money at the same time? *Start your "cottage industry" now, while you're working, just to try it out.* Here are some examples:

   - If you like to make birdhouses for your yard, make extra to sell at local craft fairs or gardening shops.

   - Perhaps you get a kick out of being around elderly people. Start your own Elder Assistant business, charging families to "visit with and assist" elderly parents for a couple of hours a week.

   - Maybe you've developed a real love of gardening and taking care of your lawn. Consider mowing lawns in your neighborhood or planting bushes, weeding, and doing other gardening tasks for neighbors for a price.

   - *The key is to think of ways to charge others to do what you love to do.*

2. **Think of creative ways to cut your expenses related to work right now.** Consider the obvious costs, like carpooling, using public transportation, and carrying your lunch to work. Reduce every expense possible connected to your current work to reap the most savings and benefit your future retirement.

3. **Open your mind to an adjusted lifestyle where you do more with less money.** You can retire sooner if you learn to live more inexpensively now.

   - Purchase generic groceries.
   - Shop farmers' markets for fresh produce.
   - Only buy meat that's on sale.
   - Concentrate on "buy one get one free" offers at the grocery store.
   - Do your shopping at a discount grocery retailer.
   - Have Meatless Mondays.
   - Be more flexible about what you choose to eat, based on what's on sale.
   - Reduce the level of cable television you pay for.
   - Get rid of your telephone land line and only pay monthly fees for your cell phone.

4. **Live in a smaller house than you can afford.** Your kids will eventually grow up and leave. *Concern yourself with living conservatively and paying off*

the mortgage after you ensure all other bills are paid off. In a smaller home, you'll live comfortably with fewer expenses.

5. **Retain part-time employment now.** Save 100% of what you earn from your second job and save it for retirement. Remind yourself daily that how you live, work, and save now will determine when you can retire and how you'll live then.

6. **Vow to learn how to delay gratification.** Go back to the old-fashioned way of living where you save up to buy something. This way, you spend only cash to get what you want. The delay in time that it will take for you to accumulate the money to pay for the item will help you determine how much you actually want the item.

When you're truly committed to a goal of retiring sooner, you'll keep your focus and follow through with these six strategies. You'll quit working before you know it and love your simpler lifestyle!

Smart Strategies for Investing During Retirement

If you're investing during retirement, you'll likely be placing a premium on immediate income generation. Investing during retirement doesn't provide you with the same luxury of time or alternative income sources like pre-retirement investing. This means that the investments themselves must yield consistent income.

If you're retired or will retire soon, you also have many other things to consider in your retirement plan, such as how to pass on value to future generations, estate planning, and how much you can safely withdraw each year without compromising your portfolio.

This guide will help you clarify your plans and realize your goals.

Consider these strategies:

1. **A dollar today will not be worth the same as a dollar tomorrow.** Inflation has shown to be a game-changer in in the economy for the past several decades and this trend shows no sign of slowing down.

   - ***It's important to consider including some medium risk investments in your portfolio to help offset the effects of inflation.*** Having too conservative of a portfolio could mean that your yearly earnings will lag behind the rate of inflation.

2. **How much can you withdraw?** This may be one of the single-most confusing areas for retirees. Often individuals approaching retirement may plan on withdrawal rates as high as 10%.

   - A more realistic number is 3% to 5%. ***By opting for a lower asset withdrawal rate, you'll be able to help ensure that you don't outlive your retirement savings.***

3. **Costs, fees and penalties.** Some companies may offer attractive-sounding fee percentages at just one or two percent. However, in some situations, these fees can amount to thousands of dollars in lost earnings.

    - Additionally, some savings have fees and penalties associated with early withdrawals and this can end up costing you a pretty penny as well. Depending on the type of account, the fees can be as high as 35%!

    - Before you invest, find out all the fees you may incur, including any for early withdrawal. Ask when would be the earliest date you could withdraw without extra costs. Then determine if this date fits your needs.

    - ***Ensuring that you understand the fees associated with your accounts can save you a considerable amount of money.***

4. **Work with an advisor.** It may be possible to do it all yourself, yet chances are you could benefit from the added experience that a trusted financial advisor brings to the table. This is not the same thing as working with a broker, which could cost you additional and unnecessary fees.

    - A financial advisor can help you navigate your retirement investing with ease. ***An advisor can also help you develop a withdrawal strategy that is both tax-efficient and helps minimize penalties or avoid them altogether.***

Investing during retirement may seem intimidating, yet it pays to be smart. ***Being aware of potential pitfalls puts you in a better position than most people,*** who base their whole retirement plans on false pretenses and inaccurate assumptions.

Whether you're currently retired or planning ahead, it's never too late to begin taking steps to maximize your earnings when investing during retirement.

Taking Responsibility for Your Financial Situation

Probably your least favorite thing to do when you're in financial hot water is to fully accept responsibility for what's happened over the last few months or years. ***It's not so much about self-blame as it is about staying keenly aware of your finances so you can take action to protect yourself.***

Perhaps you were laid off from your job or experienced a drop in your business due to the lagging economy. You might not have had much warning of what was about to happen to you financially. However – think of this: if you had been financially prepared for something like this, could your preparations have assuaged the negative impact of the crisis?

Recognize that you can take responsibility now to learn to live below your means, save for your future, and be diligent about how you spend money. In the meantime, it's wise to fully understand what your role was in getting to where you are today.

1. **What happened; how did you get here?** No, this step is not about kicking yourself. It is, however, about learning from your past experiences. ***How did you arrive at this place financially?*** Write down your answers to this question. Be very specific, thorough and brutally honest with yourself.

    - Maybe you opened every credit card account offered to you. You might have bought whatever you liked. Or you were trying to keep up with the Jones'. Did you want to impress friends?

    - Developing financial habits like eating out several times a week, buying extravagant gifts, wearing expensive clothes, and feeling like you have to have every new gadget will sooner or later cause your financial life to take a dive, unless you're doing all this while still spending less than you earn.

    - ***It's important to know the reasons for your financial condition so you won't repeat negative behaviors.*** You'll know what to correct and look out for in the future.

2. **Have you consistently paid your bills on time?** Recognize that paying your bills 100% of the time on time is very important. Why?

    - Most creditors charge fees for late payments, so **when you pay those fees, you're giving away money** you could use elsewhere, not to mention your financial reputation is harmed by not paying bills when they're due.

3. **How serious are you about changing?** It's time to ask yourself, "Why haven't I done something to better my financial situation?" Once you face the answer to that question, you can then consider how serious you are about changing your financial habits.

4. **Think positive about overhauling your financial condition.** You have the power right now to change your financial situation. Believe it, because it's true. If you commit to making whatever changes are necessary, you'll discover a better financial life – the one you deserve.

Taking responsibility for your current situation will empower you to do something about it. It might hurt at first, but to correct an error, you must acknowledge it.

Reviewing how you got into this financial state, admitting late payments, being serious about changing, and thinking positively are all necessary in your quest to take responsibility for your financial condition. Then, sooner than you might imagine, you'll realize that now you're the driving force behind a bright, secure financial future.

Rich and Staying That Way: 5 Strategies for Keeping Your Wealth

Getting rich is only half the challenge. It's not always easy to stay rich once you've 'made it.' There are many stories of very wealthy people losing everything. This includes wealthy celebrities, professional athletes, lottery winners, and lot of regular people, too.

Whether you've already made your fortune or you're still working on it, there are things that you can do to hold on to your wealth.

Protect your wealth from these five dream killers:

1. **Plan for the long-term.** As medical science continues to advance, life spans are also advancing. The more time you spend in old age, the more likely you are to have significant medical expenses. Nursing homes are very expensive, too. Plan your finances as if you were going to live forever.

   - *Research long-term care insurance and consider investing in annuities.* Annuities convert a lump sum into a monthly income for the remainder of your life.

2. **The IRS wants your money.** Those with high incomes can potentially pay much more in taxes. The IRS also wants to take a big cut when you die. Estate taxes are currently as high as 40 percent. You probably worked hard for your wealth. Avoid giving the IRS more than absolutely necessary!

   - Make full use of tax-advantaged retirement accounts like IRAs or a 401(k). Use an estate-planning attorney to help avoid estate taxes. An expert financial planner can reduce your income tax liability by putting you into tax-saving investments.

3. **Eliminate your debt.** Many people have become wealthy by taking on a lot of debt and using that money for investing or growing a business. But at some point, that money will have to be paid back. Now might be that time.

   - Reorganize your finances regularly as your situation changes. Becoming wealthy is one thing, but being wealthy and maintaining wealth is something else. Let your methods grow with your fortune.

4. **Beware of pirates.** *If you have money, you're a target.* For example, if you're middle class and get into a fender bender, it's a hassle. If the same thing happens when you're wealthy, you're potentially sending the other driver's kids through law school.

    - *Having the necessary liability coverage becomes more important as your wealth increases.* In addition to the usual insurance coverage, an umbrella liability policy is a smart move for those with deep pockets. Many people are looking for easy money. Protect yourself.

5. **Avoid unusual investments.** Warren Buffet became incredibly wealthy by investing in very ordinary types of companies, like soft-drink manufacturers and banks. You don't need to invest in a llama farm on the moon to grow your wealth. Exotic investments frequently turn out to be bad investments or even fraudulent.

    - It seems that no one is immune to seeking even greater wealth. If you already have all the money you need, then taking big risks isn't smart. Keep investing and growing, but there's no reason to expose your wealth to a lot of risk. At some point, it's time to make some adjustments to your risk tolerance.

Getting rich is challenging. Staying rich has its own set of challenges. *Spend the same amount of energy preserving your wealth as you spent creating it.* These simple steps will help.

5 Ways to Make Money Without Spending a Dime

Are you broke? Do you worry about where your next paycheck will come from? Have you been pulling your hair out due to financial stress? Many of us have those moments. ***It can be difficult to cope with a poor financial situation.***

When someone lacks money, their choices are limited. It's discouraging when there are things you want to do and you're unable to afford to do them. There's a whole world to explore, but you need cash before you can start living life to the fullest.

Wouldn't you love to learn how to make some extra money without spending it? It isn't as difficult as it sounds!

Consider these ideas to bring in extra money without having to spend some to get started:

1. **Create a service using one of your talents.** Everyone's good at something. Most of us even have a talent that can be monetized. Talents like these can be turned into profitable services: writing, website design, public speaking, playing a musical instrument, humor, singing, and much more.

    - Compile a list of your talents and see if there's a demand for any of those skills.

2. **Sell something online.** There are thousands of websites which allow people to post classified ads for free.

    - Look through your basement or storage units and make a list of items that could be sold. You can create a small business selling second hand items for a profit. This process is called "product flipping."

    - ***You can post items for sale on Craigslist and eBay.***

3. **Compile a list of services and sell them as a package.** How many times have you stumbled upon a pamphlet with a company offering a wide range of interesting services? It might be a good idea for you to combine different related services and sell them as one package.

    - For example, if you're a good writer, you could offer a range of services like writing articles, editing, proofreading websites, creating resumes, or any other service that could capitalize on your writing skills.

    - You can make a lot of money like this and it's completely free. The internet is a great way to advertise your services.

4. **Offer to babysit, housesit, or watch someone's pets while they're on vacation.** There are plenty of people who need help with these tasks and they're willing to pay well. ***Babysitting, housesitting, or watching someone's pets are great gigs for those who have extra free time.***

    - Consider creating a pamphlet offering these services. Leave them on local billboards or pass them out in your neighborhood. Remember to include a phone number!

    - Word of mouth marketing is one of the best ways to spread the word. If you do a good job, your clients will recommend you to their friends.

5. **Teach.** Everyone has knowledge that they can pass on to others. ***Figure out what you can teach and then find people who would pay to learn it.*** Teaching can be fun, rewarding, and profitable.

    - There are websites that allow members to create an online classroom and teach people a specific skill. These sites often allow teachers to charge their own rates.

    - Prepare a course on a topic that interests you and then teach it. If your students love it, they'll recommend it to others, and your business will boom.

As you can see, there are many ways to make money without having to spend it. All that's required is a touch of creativity and a "go-getter" attitude. Mix those two with determination, and you have a recipe for success. Before long, you won't have to keep worrying about how you're going to pay the bills next month. Give it a shot!

6 Wise Money Moves for Busy Boomers Who Don't Plan to Retire

Do you see yourself as someone who won't ever retire? You probably know some people who have already retired, but you can't imagine that you'd ever stop working.

As retirement age gets closer, do you identify your own thoughts about retirement in these statements?

1. **"I'm never going to retire. I can't afford it."** If you think this way, you likely haven't saved much for retirement. ***Such thoughts could become a self-fulfilling prophecy*** and you might end up working until your health fails or you're forced into retirement.

    - Either way, you're financially unprepared for the fact that you'll eventually retire.

2. **"I love my job and I want to work forever."** Although it's wonderful that you enjoy your work, that love will not stop the aging process. As years pass, the way you think will eventually change, as could your health, work situation, and environment.

3. **"My dad worked all his life and died on the job and so will I."** You believe you're a helpless pawn of fate and won't retire due to expecting an untimely death.

    - However, if you live longer than your parents (and according to statistics, you will), you may find yourself in a position to retire someday. ***The real question is, "Will you be financially ready?"***

4. **"I don't think about retiring. I guess things will turn out the way they're supposed to."** This reaction is like sticking your head into the sand and ignoring one of life's realities: if you're lucky enough to live long enough, you'll eventually retire.

What to Do Now to Prepare for Your Financial Future

By now, maybe you're considering that you'll actually retire. What can you do immediately to begin establishing a bright financial future during retirement?

Talk with your partner about the kind of life you'd want if you stopped working. ***Make some plans that make such a life possible for you.***

Ponder these tips:

1. **Accept reality.** You'll likely retire at some point. Think about your current finances and how you'd live if for some reason unknown to you today, you had to stop working tomorrow.

2. **Start saving this week.** Aim for putting back 15% of your salary. Look at it this way: it can only help you to have some extra money in the bank.

3. **Establish a retirement account.** Talk with your tax accountant about the best type of retirement account for your situation: Individual Retirement Account (IRA), Roth IRA, or a 401 (k), for example.

4. **Develop passive income resources.** *How can you get started now to establish a new source of passive income and keep it going?*

5. **Focus on building assets.** Maintain your home at the highest level. This way, if you decide to sell, your house will be in tip-top shape. Begin some short-term investments (five years or less) and regularly place some dollars there.

6. **Reduce outgoing expenditures.** Take a look at the amount of money you have going out in an average month. Look for ways to cut spending and follow through with instituting those cuts.

Regardless of your reasons for feeling you won't ever retire, start planning for a time when due to health, age, or level of physical energy, you'll at least slow down working. *Put these strategies to work, even if you don't plan to retire.* You'll be glad you did.

Avoid These Mistakes When Saving for Retirement

If you're already saving for retirement, you've taken a step in the right direction. However, there are a lot of mistakes you could still be making when it comes to retirement planning.

Making poor decisions when saving for retirement can result in having to work as a Walmart greeter to pay your bills instead of traveling the world and scratching items off of your bucket list.

To give yourself the best chance of enjoying retirement, avoid these slip-ups:

1. **Not planning at all.** There's a saying that goes "If you fail to plan, you plan to fail." *If you want to have enough money to live comfortably during your retirement, start planning now.* The sooner you start the better.

   - An easy way to start planning for your retirement is to simply take part in any retirement plan offered by your employer. It may be a pension, a 401(k), or some other program.

2. **Leaving free money on the table.** Many employers have a program in place where they'll match a certain percentage of whatever their employees invest in their retirement funds.

   - *To avoid leaving free money on the table, ensure you contribute enough money to your 401(k) to take full advantage of the maximum that your employer will match.*

3. **Depending too heavily on Social Security.** The amount of money you'll receive in Social Security benefits depends largely on how much you paid into it. The average person in 2023 can expect to receive somewhere around $18,600 per year. ($1,500 per month)

   - If $18,600 per year isn't enough to cover your expenses, you may want to look into investing in a 401(k), a Roth IRA, or some other personal investment account.

4. **Having no idea how much money you need to save for retirement.** It's important to calculate how much money you may need to live comfortably during your retirement in order to get an idea of how much to save and invest each month.

    - *Knowing how much money to save before you reach retirement age can give you the motivation to start socking away some extra cash every month.* Knowledge is power!

5. **Retiring with a mountain of debt.** If you can pay off all of your outstanding debts before you retire, it will be a lot easier to get by on a fixed income.

6. **Underestimating healthcare costs.** The cost of healthcare seems to go up each year. As you get older, the chances that you'll need healthcare increase as well.

    - *Research conducted by Fidelity in 2022 showed that an average 65-year-old couple would need approximately $315,000 (after tax) to cover their medical expenses throughout their retirement.* This figure is over and above anything that Medicare would pay for.

These are some of the biggest blunders people often make when planning for retirement. In addition to these mistakes, if you're invested in the stock market, beware of overreacting to market volatility or having a lack of diversity in your investments.

Whether you've invested in the stock market or just have a 401(k) through your employer, it may be a good idea to consult with a financial planner who can help with your retirement planning.

Do You Struggle with Compulsive Spending?

Compulsive spending involves feeling compelled to spend money on items you don't really want or need. In some cases, you might spend money on items you already have plenty of. For example, even though you love getting new shoes, if you already have 20 pairs of them, it's probably safe to say you don't need another.

Signs You May Be Spending Compulsively

Do any of these signs feel familiar?

1. **You spend all your money as soon as you get it.** On payday, you might pay some bills. Then, any money you have left over, you happily go out to spend. Maybe there's a big clearance on home improvement tools or the dress boutique is having a going out of business sale. Whatever the case, you deplete the monies you obtain.

2. **You use charge cards to buy items when you have no money.** A financially dangerous habit, ***using charge cards to keep buying once the cash is gone can devastate your money and living situations.***

3. **You shop when you feel moody, anxious, or upset in some way.** Your feelings largely depend on whether you're shopping, since shopping comforts you during any stress.

4. **You feel your spending is out of control.** No matter what you do, you just can't stop.

5. **Your shopping causes difficulties in your life.** You perhaps have arguments with your spouse about all the money you spend. Sometimes, you aren't honest about what you spent.

How to Stop

If you experience even one of these points above, there's a real possibility you're dealing with compulsive spending.

Use these strategies to quell your urges to spend:

1. **Make a contract with yourself to stop spending.** Write it out and sign it. Find the confidence to change your direction.

2. **For now, remove credit cards from your wallet.** If you believe you have the fortitude to use a credit card only for emergencies, keep only 1 card in your billfold. Pay cash for everything. Budget your daily cash amount and when you run out of cash, you're done spending (on anything) for the rest of the day.

3. **Contemplate your money situation.** How long has it been going on? How did you get started spending compulsively? Are there specific situations that trigger you to shop now? How do you feel when spending money? *Work hard to gain an understanding of your drive to spend compulsively.*

4. **Charge yourself for spending.** Every time you spend money for something other than groceries, gas, or utility bills, pay yourself $20.00. This means you must put back the $20.00 to have ready when the bill for the frivolous items comes in.

5. **Write down all expenditures.** *When you see on paper the amount you spent and what you spent it for, it somehow becomes real.* In a sense, you're forcing yourself to think about and process what you're doing.

6. **Examine the possessions you already have.** Do you like and use all of them? If you have several debts due to your past credit card spending, think about how you can return or re-sell some of the items you've purchased haphazardly. Then, use that money to pay off the debts.

7. **Recognize spending money doesn't buy you happiness.** Be honest with yourself: has surrounding yourself with stuff you bought with your hard-earned money provided you the life you truly seek?

8. **Empower yourself** by becoming more conscious about how spending affects your life. List the ways your life would change if you had no debt and used money wisely.

9. **Make contact with the Debtors Anonymous group in your area.** Asking for help is the wise thing to do whenever you believe your spending is out of control. Going to Debtors Anonymous won't cost a dime and can provide support for you to get your life back on track.

If you've identified yourself as one who spends compulsively, you've taken a first step in the right direction. Making a contract, avoiding credit cards, charging yourself for spending, keeping track of expenditures, and returning or re-selling unused purchased items will help you get a grip.

Also, listing how your life will change when you stop spending, realizing spending doesn't make you happy, and going to Debtors Anonymous will set you on a positive path to real emotional and financial freedom.

How to Live Successfully Without a Car

Unless you live in a major metropolitan area with great public transportation, you probably have an automobile. It might seem impossible to survive in the United States without a car, but many people successfully do exactly that.

A car is an expensive item that carries a lot of costs beyond the sales price: gasoline, maintenance, repairs, insurance and parking. ***There's also the opportunity cost.*** That money could be invested toward your retirement.

If you're truly interested in retiring early, getting rid of your car can be powerful decision.

Try these tips for living successfully without a car:

1. **Consider all the times you use a car now.** It's likely to be for work, shopping, vacations, carting around the kids, and perhaps church.

2. **Develop a list of alternatives.** For example, you could find a nearby coworker and offer to split the gas cost for a ride to and from work each day. Public transportation is another option. You might be able to find a friend or neighbor that's willing to let you borrow their car.

   - ***Ridesharing has vastly improved over the last few years.*** There are phone apps that make it quick and easy to find a ride on short notice. With the popularity of social networks and GPS, the process is much more robust and convenient than it has been in the past. Give it a try before your decide it's not for you.

   - You could always ride a bike. It's a great way to save money for retirement and get in great shape! Walking is another option.

   - Many stores are offering free delivery now. You might be able to shop online and have your groceries brought to your house for free. No more waiting in line or driving in bad weather.

3. **Remind yourself of the reasons you're getting rid of your car.** It can be challenging to sacrifice in the present for some future benefit. It's not easy to diet in January to get ready for the summer either. Whenever you're feeling frustrated, keep the end in mind.

4. **Ensure you're getting the benefit.** It's easy to spend all the money you're saving on other things. ***Remember to take that money and invest it.*** According to AAA, the average cost of owning a mid-size car is almost $10,000 per year.

- Calculate the full cost of owning your car and make an effort to invest a similar amount this year. Remember that you're still going to have some costs associated with alternate transportation.
5. **If getting rid of your car is simply too much, consider a compromise.** Most families own two or more cars. Many families and singles own nicer cars than necessary. If you're unable to survive without a car, there's a compromise that can still save a ton of money.

    - *Limit your household to a single, economical car.* Avoid automobiles that get poor gas mileage or have a poor reliability rating. It's very common for today's vehicles to last for at least 200,000 miles. A car with 100,000 miles is barely middle-aged, but the same car can be bought at a fraction of the original price.

If you don't live in a large metropolitan area, life without a car can be challenging. But people are doing it successfully. *At the very least, consider downsizing your current car situation.* Cars are very expensive and all that money could be used to secure your early retirement. If you're serious about early retirement, seriously examine the option of living without a car.

How to Prepare for Financial Challenges

Financial concerns have the potential to keep us awake at night. Unfortunately, most of us wait until a crisis is upon us before we get busy. ***Do what's best for you and your family and prepare now.*** You'll sleep better at night knowing that you have plans in place for contingencies.

Begin using these strategies now — *before* a financial challenge arises — and you'll lessen its negative impact on your life:

1. **Have sufficient savings.** Set aside enough money in things like checking and savings accounts, money market accounts, and short-term certificates of deposit to cover 3-6 months of living expenses. You should have this in place before you begin investing money elsewhere.

    - Some benefits of these accounts are that they don't fluctuate with market conditions, and there is no tax penalty for withdrawing the money, unlike retirement accounts.

2. **Make a budget.** If you don't already have a budget, there's no time like the present to get started. ***The first step to making a real change is to measure where you're at right now.***

    - Developing a budget will provide you with the information you really need to take control of your spending and free up funds for saving.

3. **Consider how you would reduce your monthly expenses.** You don't have to make changes now, but take a look at your monthly bills and see where you could alter your spending *if you needed to*. You'll feel most financially secure with a plan already in place.

4. **Be aggressive with your bills.** Get organized and sit down with all your bills twice a month to pay the bills that are coming due. Many families waste money every month in late fees and other penalties.

    - ***Make a list of all your bills and their due dates.*** Review as needed to ensure that you pay on time.

5. **Reduce your credit card debt.** Credit card interest can really eat into your budget every month. If you have your emergency savings taken care of, this is now the best place to put any extra money after your expenses have been worked into your budget.

6. **Find a less expensive credit card.** If the interest rate is high on your current card, shop around and see what you can find. You may be able to receive a zero interest offer for balance transfers or a greatly reduced interest rate, at least to start with.

    - *Never pay more interest than you have to.* However, be sure to read the fine print with any credit card offering.

7. **Earn some extra cash.** Sell some of the stuff in the garage, attic, or basement that you don't really need and use the extra cash to build up your savings or pay off credit card debt.

    - *Establish a second income source.* This is especially handy if you happen to lose the first.

8. **Review your insurance coverage.** Are you getting the best deals? Shopping around and comparing policies is time well spent. Also consider disability insurance if you don't already have it. Ask yourself if you'll be able to pay all your bills if you're sick or injured and can't even get out of bed.

Don't wait until a financial challenge comes into your life, instead, begin your preparations now and avoid the stress.

Financial hiccups happen to everyone, but those who are ready for them are better able to get back on their feet quickly. Get started now and you'll sleep like a baby while others are up late worrying about financial disaster.

Preparing for Early Retirement: Tax Implications of Your Money-Making Hobby

There's no doubt that a moneymaking hobby can dramatically reduce the amount of time until retirement. **Not only can you sock away more money, you can also use that income during your retirement.** This reduces the amount that you need to save prior to retirement. Since hobbies are enjoyable, it's a win-win situation.

But like most other income, income from your hobby is also taxable. Taxes are a considerable expense, so they should be minimized, when possible.

This is a touchy issue for the IRS. Many people try to deduct losses for activities that are primarily conducted for enjoyment. It's easy to get yourself into trouble.

Hobby Tax Tips

1. **For tax purposes, understand what "hobby" means.** The IRS considers a hobby to be an activity that is done primarily for enjoyment, not for making a profit. If your activity is considered to be a hobby, you can't use the tax deductions available to legitimate business. However, you will be taxed for profit and can deduct your expenses in the same year.

    - For example, if you bought $1,000 in rare coins and didn't earn any income, you couldn't deduct the $1,000 from your other income. However, if you sold the coins for $1,200, you would be taxed on the $200 profit, provided you sold the coins in the same tax year they were purchased.

2. **Hobbies are terrible for tax purposes.** It's important to create a business for your hobby. **Think business, not hobby.** If you expect to make a profit, and your expectation is considered to be reasonable, then you can consider your hobby to be a business. There is more information available from the IRS here.

    - There is no advantage to not declaring your hobby a business if your intention is to earn income. **When it comes to the IRS, remove the word hobby from your vocabulary.**

3. **Consider hiring your non-working family members.** Remember that no income tax has to be paid below a certain income threshold. Paying your children or non-working spouse a salary to help you with your business is a great way to avoid income taxes.

    - Paying your spouse keeps the money in your collective pockets. Paying your children provides a great way to save money for college, tax-free. Ideally, you would be in the position to pay both.

4. **If your goal really is early retirement, consider investing the profits in tax-deferred retirement accounts.** Depending on how much income you earn, your options will vary. But at the very least, an IRA makes a lot of sense. You can shield your income from taxes, at least temporarily.

    - A Roth-IRA requires after-tax income, but the earnings are tax-free. A traditional IRA uses pre-tax income, but the earnings are taxed.

IRAs are great, but remember the money is out of your hands until the standard retirement age. If you want to retire early and need that money, be sure to invest the money wisely. Avoid spending the extra income on other things.

Learn how to run a business wisely. There are a plethora of books and other sources that will provide the information needed to run a business effectively. ***Maximize your income for the amount of time you want to dedicate to your hobby.*** Don't hesitate to get expert tax advice, too.

A moneymaking hobby can be an important part of any early retirement plan. Think about the things you like to do and make a list of ways you can make money from those activities. But take the steps to avoid paying more taxes than necessary.

Financial Strategies Regarding Divorce in Retirement

Discover How to Survive a Divorce with Your Finances Intact

Divorce can be devastating, both emotionally and financially. ***It's a delicate time that can easily result in making poor decisions.*** These decisions can have an impact on your finances for a long period of time. Making wise decisions can shorten the time it takes to recover financially.

Fortunately, many of the things that need to be done after a divorce don't require a lot of thought. Some choices are easy to make.

Follow these strategies to get your finances in order after divorce:

1. **Open your own bank account and close any joint accounts.** If you're getting divorced, you don't want to be stuck with any financial liabilities your soon-to-be ex creates. This doesn't just include bank accounts. Any credit cards are also potential nightmares. Contact your bank and credit card companies and explain the situation.

    - Open new accounts in just your name. This might be easier to do before closing the joint accounts. ***Ensure that you'll have access to money throughout the divorce process.***

2. **Consider your housing situation.** This can be greatly complicated by the presence of children. Otherwise, it's often easier to sell the home and move on. When children are part of the picture, it's often best to consult with an attorney to examine your options.

3. **Be aware of all your assets.** Do you know the full extent of your financial holdings during your marriage? In many cases, one spouse handles the financial matters, and the other is happy to stay out of it. ***Now is the time to dig in and develop an accurate picture of what you have.*** You might be surprised by what you discover.

    - Now you have to collectively decide how to handle the assets. Do you split them? Sell them and split the proceeds? Or hire a lawyer and battle it out?

4. **Take a look at all your insurance needs.** You might need to get on your own medical insurance plan. What items do you still own that need to be insured? Your insurance costs might be much less now. There's no reason to carry more insurance than you need.

    - ***Your situation has changed, so your insurance needs have likely changed as well.***

5. **Create a new budget.** You income and expenses have changed, so it only makes sense that your budget will change too. If you've gone from a two-income

household to a single income, there's likely less margin for error. Create a budget that makes sense for your new circumstances.

6. **Change beneficiaries on your life insurance and retirement accounts.** There's a good chance that your beneficiary was your spouse. You'll probably want to list new beneficiaries. For most accounts, this is easily accomplished by filling out a simple form. This step is often overlooked.

- *Ensure that, in the event of your death, your assets go to those whom you want to have them.*

7. **Get a copy of your credit report.** It's important to know where you stand financially. It's just as important to be aware of all of your accounts. Your spouse may have opened a joint account or credit card without your knowledge. The better your credit, the easier it is to move through the world.

Divorce is a difficult time for all. **But a divorce can be especially difficult if financial matters are not handled intelligently.** Focusing your attention on housing, debt, income, and assets will make the transition easier.

These tips highlight the basics. In many instances, an attorney will be required. But understanding the basic issues will make it easier to make wise decisions. Apply these strategies to your circumstances and get the professional guidance you require.

You'll Be Okay: Financially Adjusting to Divorce

Are you going through a marital breakup? If so, you might feel like you're in a whirlwind. You're worried. Will you be okay financially? Take a look at the following points to recognize you'll likely make it through, with a few adjustments here and there.

1. **Do the math.** Figure out if you can support yourself financially with the dollars you now earn. ***Remember to include other funds that will be coming in, like child support, alimony, or stock dividends.***

2. **Act now.** If you're going to need a new or different job or additional income, start doing something about it now. If you begin bringing in additional dollars right away, it'll take some of the pressure off later.

3. **Determine monthly expenses.** How much are your monthly outgoing expenditures? Can you count your basic expenditures on one hand: mortgage or rent, car payment, utility bill, food costs, and phone/internet charges?

   - For the other hand, you'll have insurance, entertainment, and savings. ***If you have a lot of monthly payments like 2 or 3 credit cards and more than one car payment, it's time to consider some spending cuts.***

4. **Don't panic.** If you need to make some reductions, decide what you'll cut out. Maybe you can sell one of the cars to eliminate a car payment and reduce your car insurance. Perhaps you'll decrease cell phone charges or cut out paying for your phone land line.

   - Maybe you can combine your 2 or 3 credit card payments all onto one card for 1 monthly payment for everything you owe. If you must, cancel your Netflix account or whatever extra accounts you can do without, at least for now.

   - ***Once you have your expenses under control and know how your money situation will be, you can add back services you want.***

5. **Take an honest look.** Are you living equal to or below your means financially? Do you and your child really need to live in a 2,700 square foot home? Or could you be perfectly happy in a home that's half the size? Consider this: you'd be paying half the electric bill (you now pay) every month plus lower rent.

    - Once you get some time as a single person under your belt, you can upgrade your standards later.

    - The point is to ensure you're not living right up to the edge of what you make. If you are, it can make for a rather nerve-wracking life. ***With some planning, you might be able to reduce your expenses and still live a financially comfortable life.***

6. **Heads up regarding your tax return.** If you're not yet divorced as of the last day of the year (12/31), you can still file jointly if you both agree to do so. Also, if you'll have custody of your children the most, ensure your attorney declares in your divorce decree that you can claim them as dependents.

    - If you're paying alimony, have your attorney include that in your decree. This way, you can claim the amount you pay as a tax deduction.

7. **Take care when splitting up retirement funds.** This issue gets sticky. Talk with your attorney about the best way to handle such funds because, depending on your age and how you do it, you might have to pay early withdrawal fees plus taxes on the withdrawn amount. There are ways to do it without paying these penalties.

When it comes to making it through a divorce financially, recognize millions of people have survived it and you can, too. Recall the toughest times you've had and realize the financial smarts you possess to get through. If you follow the above suggestions, you'll be well on your way to successfully surviving the financial consequences of a divorce. You'll be okay.

How to Eliminate Money Arguments in Your Marriage

Marital arguments about money have been going on since the invention of money. While all arguments can take their toll, disagreements over finances can be particularly distressing. ***Studies show that money issues are among the leading causes of divorce!*** This is a worthwhile subject to get under control. Not only will your finances improve, but your marriage will strengthen, too.

These steps can keep money arguments to a minimum:

1. **Agree on a budget.** Many couples don't have a budget, but a budget is useful for everyone, even billionaires. ***If you can both agree on a spending plan, many potential arguments can be avoided.*** After all, if someone is outspending the budget, it's difficult to argue about fault.

    - It's practically impossible to get a budget right on the first attempt. ***Good budgets evolve over a few months.*** It will take some tinkering to get it right. Be patient and make the necessary adjustments as you go along.

    - Use the information you already have. Pull out old bills and use some real numbers. Remember to consider expenses that occur less frequently than once a month. New tires, home repairs, and medical expenses are just a few ideas.

2. **Be completely open.** Many couples are exactly sure how much money their spouse is making. Many more spouses are in the dark about their partner's debt and credit history. It's not always easy, but a full financial disclosure can prevent many disagreements.

    - ***Knowing each other's financial status will make it easier to agree on a financial plan.***

    - This includes being honest about all spending. More than a few women hide clothing and shoe purchases from their spouse in the back of the closet. More than a few men buy tools on a regular basis and sneak them into the garage. Be honest.

3. **Set financial goals together.** ***If you're both working toward the same things, it will bring you closer together.*** Partnership and marriage go hand in hand. Sharing a vision is an effective way of limiting arguments.

    - Sit down together and dream big about the future. Then decide how that looks financially. What plans will you have to make? How will you accomplish them? Set a deadline and get busy.

4. **Deal with discrepancies in pay.** In most cases, one spouse has a greater salary than the other. Splitting the bills 50:50 might be fair in one context, but it can also create resentment. One option is to pay the bills relative to the salaries. So, if one person is making $100k, and the other is making $50k, the bills would be split 2/3 and 1/3.

5. **Deal with discrepancies in expenses and debt.** If one spouse has child support payments to make or a large amount of student loan debt, the other might want to consider making adjustments for this when dealing with the bills. Partners help each other out. ***If you want to share in the windfalls, it's only fair to share with the less agreeable things, too.***

6. **Handle disagreements in a healthy manner.** Disagreements will occur, no matter how good the intentions. It's important to keep the discussion centered on behaviors and not people. There's a difference between, *"This purchase wasn't within our budget"* and *"You ruined our budget."*

   - When a disagreement occurs, find a solution that will prevent a reoccurrence.

Minimizing money-related arguments is a great way to strengthen a marriage. ***It's also a great way to get your finances under control.*** Many of the steps involved will encourage healthy finances. Protect your marriage and do what's necessary to eliminate money arguments.

Habits of Financially Successful Singles

Some of us enjoy being single and some of us don't. But there's no arguing with the fact that being single can be more financially challenging. ***An additional income is a great advantage, and two people have relatively similar living expenses as a single person.*** Being single means having to pay for everything yourself.

If you're living life as a single, consider adopting these financial habits:

1. **Limit the size of your home to match your budget.** Only requiring a one-bedroom apartment to satisfy your living space needs is one advantage of being single. It can be tempting to try to compete with your married friends. After all, many of them are likely to have nice homes. Resist this urge and limit your housing to what you really need.

    - Most people spend 90% of their time at home in the bedroom, kitchen, and living room anyway. You can do all of that in a small home or apartment and save your money for more important things.

2. **Successful singles take advantage of being the sole decision maker. *Being single means having the freedom to make decisions without having to accommodate the desires of others.*** It also means there isn't anyone there to keep you honest. Take the time to make good financial decisions. Take advantage of the fact that you're in control.

    - Being married means having to consider the needs and desires of another adult. There is always compromise.

3. **Travel with a friend.** If you don't have a significant other, traveling can be much more expensive. This is mostly due to paying for accommodations by yourself. In general, a hotel room for two costs the same as a room for a single. Consider going on vacation with a friend or review vacations designed for singles.

    - There are also many options today to minimize lodging costs. Do a search online and you'll be surprised at the many ways to reduce these costs.

4. **Pay yourself first.** This is an excellent habit for anyone, but it's especially important for singles. ***The need for an emergency fund is greater for singles.*** You're the only person paying into it. If a real financial challenge appears, you're the only one available to handle it. Pay yourself first so you're ready for anything.

5. **Take care of business at work.** With a single income, the loss of a job can be especially challenging. If things aren't going well at work, either fix them or start looking for new employment. Many of us do just the minimum at work to avoid being fired.

- If possible, consider nurturing a part-time second income that accommodates your lifestyle.
6. **Start saving for retirement immediately.** If you stay single, you'll be your only source of retirement savings and investment. You might not plan on staying single, but it's better to be safe than sorry. Besides, saving for retirement is an excellent habit for anyone.

While being single has its challenges, it also has many benefits. You alone control your finances and can make all the decisions. ***The responsibility is on you to make smart choices.*** Minimize your expenses where you can. It's all about saving, protecting your income, and being prepared for the future. Begin adopting the habits of financially successful singles today.

Vacation Tips

7 Tips to Save Money on Your Next Vacation

The travel options most of us are exposed to are expensive. It's unlikely that you'll see many advertisements for budget vacations. ***The travel destinations you see in colorful brochures, high-end magazines, and on television are run by high-profit travel companies.*** While those vacations are a possibility, there are more economical options to consider.

Many people manage to travel the world on a budget of $50 or less per day!

Take advantage of these strategies and save money on your next vacation:

1. **Try the shoulder season.** Hitting Europe in the summer and Aruba in the winter might be ideal. However, you can save a lot of money by traveling just before or after peak seasons. The costs are lower and the weather is still good. It's also less crowded and more peaceful.

2. **Bid for your hotel room.** Most travelers are aware of websites like Priceline.com and Hotwire.com. But, it's challenging to know if you're getting the best deal.

   - Betterbidding.com can provide actual bidding information and advice for the popular bidding websites. You can find out the average room rate and compare. Then, you'll know with certainty if you're bidding too little or too much.

3. **Wait until the last minute.** *While airfares go through the roof close to the travel date, many other travel-related services, like cruises and tours, tend to drop in price.*

   - Why is that? Who flies at the last minute? Typically people on business-related travel. This group of travelers isn't as price conscious.

   - Cruises and tours mostly have fixed costs, so they get all the money upfront. There's little reason to send out a cruise ship with empty rooms. Leaving those rooms vacant gets them zero dollars, so they'd rather sell trips at a discount to bring in more income.

4. **Plan your meals.** It's easy to spend a lot of money on food, especially if you have a large family. Find discount coupons and deals ahead of time. Decide where you're going to eat before starting on your journey.

   - Remember that you can cook for yourself, too, even on vacation, with some advance planning. An electric skillet can save you a lot when you're on vacation!

5. **Travel light.** Airlines like to give the impression of lower fares, but by now you likely know the truth. They charge for everything else that used to be free. And bags cost a fortune. Some airlines charge for any checked luggage. Plus, overweight bags can cost you literally *hundreds* of extra dollars before you even board the plane for your trip!

6. **If you're taking a road trip, consider your gas consumption.** *There are many rewards programs that can help you save money on gas.* If you have a smart phone, you can find apps to assist you with finding the best gas prices on your route. Many gift cards give additional discounts on gasoline, as well.

7. **Find free entertainment.** Most cities have some sort of free entertainment just about every day of the week. Many museums offer free admission one day a week. Get online and see what's happening where you're vacationing.

A budget vacation doesn't have to feel like you're skimping. It simply requires some creative planning. *With a concerted effort, you can have your greatest vacation ever, without breaking the bank.*

Use these tips and your own ideas to save money while giving your family a vacation to remember.

What If... You Had a Vacation with No Bills?

Do the sweet memories of your vacation tarnish a bit when you start getting the credit card bills for it the month after you return home, or as you spend a year paying off your trip from *last* year? Imagine how differently you would feel if there were no bills to come home to!

The best way to steer clear of anxiety and guilt is to save for your trip before ever heading out the door. This will result in a more enjoyable vacation because you'll already have the money set aside and won't have to worry.

It's easy to save for a vacation if you set a goal, cut back on your spending, and save money on a regular basis.

Follow these tips to budget and save for your next vacation:

1. **Agree on a goal.** Get together with the family and agree on a vacation destination. Saving is rarely exciting, but once it's attached to an objective, it becomes tolerable.

2. **Develop a vacation budget.** If you want to save painlessly, a budget helps. Based on your destination, create a reasonable budget. Be certain to include everything. If someone needs to care for your dog and cut your grass, include it. Take the time to be accurate.

3. **Calculate a weekly goal.** Divide your budget by the number of weeks until your vacation. That's how much you need to save each week. ***Saving weekly makes it easier to get back on track if you miss a target.*** If you're an entire month behind, it's more challenging to get caught up.

4. **Find ways to "create" some excess money.** Make a detailed list of your monthly expenses and see where you can cut back. Everyone buys things that are "wants" rather than needs.

    - Food is one area where most families spend too much. Avoid eating out more than necessary and make an effort to shop more economically. Packaged foods tend to be more expensive than the healthier alternatives.

    - ***Consider ditching your landline or any other service you don't really use.*** You, your spouse, and maybe even your children have cell phones. Do you need a landline, too? What about that gym membership? Are you using it regularly?

    - Look at the loans you're carrying. If you haven't checked the interest rates lately, you might be able to save a significant amount by refinancing.

5. **Put away the money you save on cutting back.** It's one thing to cut your cell phone bill or loan payment down. It's another to actually take that $50 and set it aside so it won't be spent. Create a savings account and simply transfer the money you've saved into it each week.

    - Consider having some money automatically transferred into a "vacation savings account" each month.

    - *Try throwing all your change into a jar at the end of each day and deposit it into your vacation account whenever it gets full.*

6. **Assess your progress.** Regularly check on the status of your savings. Look at the calendar and see how you're doing in regards to your savings target. *Then, make any necessary changes.*

Saving for a vacation can be easy and painless. It all starts with a goal and a budget. With those two items in place, you can determine how much you need to save and implement your plan. Have the best vacation ever without having to worry about spending outside your means!

Strategies to Reduce Expenses in Retirement

9 Ways to Cut Prescription Costs

Everything related to medical care is expensive.

Medical expenses are responsible for well over 60% of the bankruptcy filings in the United States. Prescriptions can be a significant expense with some pharmaceuticals can cost over $1,000 a week!

If you don't have comprehensive insurance, paying for your medications can be a real challenge.

Use these strategies to reduce your prescription costs:

1. **Get the generic.** Anytime your doctor writes a prescription, ask if there is a generic equivalent. Generics can be much less expensive and some pharmacies will fill many generic prescriptions for $4! Most of us can afford $4.

2. **Ask for price matching.** Sometimes your pharmacy will match the price at another pharmacy, even if that other pharmacy does business strictly via mail order. Pharmacies are competitive, just like any other business. It never hurts to ask.

3. **Get a phone app.** There are phone apps that will compare the cost of your prescription at multiple pharmacies in your area. There are several, just do a search and find one that works for you.

4. **Split the pills.** Many medications cost about the same, regardless of dosage. So you might be able to buy the prescription at double strength and split the tablets with a pill splitter. You just saved 50% on the cost of your medication.

5. **Cut coupons.** There are also coupons for many medications. Check the magazines in your doctor's waiting room. You can also look at these websites: www.internetdrugcoupons.com and www.optimizerx.com.

6. **Find a new pharmacy.** Pharmacies frequently offer gift cards as an incentive for transferring a prescription to their store. Of course, you'll need to make sure you're not going to pay a lot more for the prescription. Shop around and see what's out there.

7. **Get it online.** There are many online pharmacies that tend to be significantly less expensive than local pharmacies. This makes sense, since they don't have stores and all the related expenses that go along with them.

    - What about Canadian pharmacies, where prescriptions cost about 50% less? The FDA doesn't approve of using this option, and it's technically illegal to have pharmaceuticals shipped into the country. The FDA claims safety concerns, while others claim it's merely the pharmaceutical companies flexing their muscles.

    - The website www.legitscript.com can tell you if an online pharmacy meets the legal requirements of US law.

8. **Ask for free samples.** Pharmaceutical sales reps often provide free samples to physicians. In fact, some physicians refuse to talk to reps unless they provide free samples. It never hurts to ask.

9. **Apply for free medications.** Medications are frequently made available to those of lower income. You can find low-cost and no-cost prescriptions at www.needymeds.org. If you don't have insurance, you're likely to get at least some relief.

There are many options available to reduce your prescription expense.

In many cases, prescriptions can be obtained for a greatly reduced cost compared to what you might be paying now. There is even the possibility of getting your meds for free if you can prove financial need.

If you're having a financial challenge with your meds, there are solutions. Use the above tips to lower your costs and keep more money in your bank account.

5 Costly Surprises of Retirement

Most of us think that retirement is likely to be relatively inexpensive. After all, the house and car will probably be paid-off and the kids should be gone.

However, there are several expenses that you might not consider before it's too late.

Plan ahead and don't be surprised by the following 5 expenses:

1. Health care expenses: According to the data, the average 65 year old couple will require $400,000 out of pocket to deal with medical expenses from retirement to age 92. While parts of Medicare are free, other parts are not. Parts B and D, which cover outpatient services and prescriptions are not inexpensive. It can be $6,500 a year for a couple.

- If you have a higher income, expect these premiums to be even higher. The cost isn't the same for everyone.

- Remember that long-term costs like nursing homes aren't covered either, regardless of income.

- Be sure to look at all of your health care and insurance options before retiring.

2. Greater spending: You might have your house paid off, but what are you going to do with all of that free time?

- When you're working, you don't have time to spend a lot of money. When you're retired, you might want to do things that you never had the time for. Going to the movies, playing golf, dining out, traveling, and other hobbies and entertainment aren't free.

- It's important to think about what your life will be like during retirement. From this ideal vision, you should be able to develop a reasonable budget. Are your financial assets going to be able to support this lifestyle? What can you do now to plan ahead?

- If you're used to having a company car, cell phone, or other perks, you're going to have to pay for these things yourself. The cost of former perks can be considerable.

3. Social security taxes: Nearly every working person understands that they're paying into social security. What you might not know, though, is that you're likely to be taxed again when you receive that money back in Social Security benefits. The income threshold before taxes kick-in is quite low – about $16,000 for an individual. Be prepared.

4.	Tax-deferred accounts: You didn't have to pay taxes on the income that you put into your 401(k) or traditional IRA. Unfortunately, you will have to pay taxes on your withdrawals. Adding to the misfortune, the withdrawals are taxed at your top ordinary income tax rate. This is probably more than the capital gains rate.

•	So, if you want to buy a $25,000 boat, you might have to withdraw $30,000+ from your retirement accounts to cover both the boat and the taxes.

•	This is one of the reasons that Roth IRAs are so attractive to those that qualify. With a Roth IRA, you contribute after-tax monies but your withdrawals are tax-free. That means all the growth inside the account is tax-fee also. Check with your tax professional to see if you qualify.

5.	Loss of income for the surviving spouse: At some point, one spouse is usually forced to survive without the benefits and income that came from the other spouse. The social security survivor benefit will not completely replace the lost income. Be sure that your estate planning covers the situation of a surviving spouse.

Retirement has its own set of expenses that must be taken into consideration. It's important to plan for these expenses while there's still time to make the necessary adjustments to your retirement plan. Be prepared and enjoy your retirement fully.

10 Things That Are Better to Buy Used

Everyone likes to buy new stuff, but sometimes it makes a lot of sense to purchase used items. ***Many things are much less expensive – but just as nice – when you buy them used instead of new.***

Here are 10 items that are smarter to purchase used:

1. **Your pets.** With all the animals that are readily available, it doesn't make sense to spend several hundred dollars or more on a pure bred puppy. 3.5 million dogs and cats are euthanized every year.

    - ***If you just have to own a pure bred animal, you'll be happy to know that 25% of shelter animals are pure bred.***

2. **Books.** The library is actually your best bet – it's free! Used bookstores are popular, and there are even used bookstores online. That includes textbooks, too. Plus, selling back your books and textbooks when you're done makes their final cost even less!

3. **Bicycles.** New models come out every year and last year's model will always be marked down. There are also a ton of used bikes for sale that haven't seen a lot of use.

4. **Your home.** ***Existing construction is usually considerably less expensive per square foot than new construction.*** Many new homes actually lose value over the first couple of years. So finding a nice home in an established area can save you lots of money.

5. **Children's clothing.** This is especially true for baby clothes. The clothes are barely worn before they're outgrown. Some are never worn at all. Used clothing stores are everywhere, and you can save a bundle.

    - Remember to ask co-workers, friends, and family: ***the best clothes are free clothes!***

6. **Furniture.** Many folks don't want to take their practically new furniture with them when they move. Check Craigslist and look at your local classifieds for yard sales and great deals.

7. **Vehicles.** A car that's a year old with 10,000 miles on the odometer can be as much as 30% less than a new car and still has plenty of time left on the warranty, too.

8. **Toys.** Used toys are widely available at a fraction of the cost of new toys. Keep your eyes open and you'll be pleasantly surprised. Look for them at children's resale shops and yard sales.

9. **Jewelry.** New jewelry is much more expensive than used. ***You could get a great piece for 50% less than new.***

10. **Tools.** Most tools don't get a lot of use. If you're not in a hurry, you're likely to find any tool you need for a lot less money. Flea markets, yard sales, pawnshops, and the classifieds always have used tools for sale. Remember to check estate sales as well.

Don't be afraid to purchase used items. Be knowledgeable about what you're buying and you'll be satisfied with your purchase. ***The keys to getting a really great deal are being aware of what things are really worth and being patient.***

If you'll get out there and look around, you're sure to find a great deal. You might even enjoy the process.

Which State Offers You The Best Tax Advantages for Your Retirement?

Ah, retirement. Fun in the sun, golf, and lemonade by the pool are the dream of every working person. While you're welcome to retire anywhere you want, **where you choose to retire can have a significant effect on your finances and retirement lifestyle.**

The right state for your retirement will depend on your level and sources of income. Different states have different tax laws that can really make a difference in the amount of money you'll have left over in your pocket at the end of each month. It's financially smart to consider your financial situation and sources of retirement income before you choose.

During retirement, determining your best taxation situation depends on more than just seeing if your state has a state income tax or not. For example, your favorite state might have a state income tax, but not tax pension income. So, if pension income is your main source of income, it might still benefit you financially to consider that state.

Let's look at the 4 main taxes different states apply to varying degrees:

1. **Taxes on Pension Income.** Currently, there are only three states that don't tax pension income. Those states are Mississippi, Illinois, and Pennsylvania. If you have a military or government pension, there are several more tax-free options: New York, Michigan, Hawaii, Kansas, Louisiana, Massachusetts, and Alabama.

    - ***Other states tax your pension income to varying degrees.*** Do your homework if you receive a pension as part of your retirement income.

2. **Sales Taxes.** If you don't want to pay any sales tax, then Alaska, New Hampshire, Oregon, and Montana are your answer. Of course, sales tax rates vary from state to state. Also, some states exempt certain items like food and medical care / medical supplies. Take a look before you make the leap.

    - The more you like to shop, the more sales tax will detract from your bottom line.

3. **Property Taxes.** If you own an expensive home or multiple properties, property taxes can be significant. Property taxes are largely a function of property values, so ***you can limit your property taxes by living in an area with lower real estate prices.***

    - Keep in mind that city and local taxes can be a significant portion of property taxes. Find out what you can expect to pay in property taxes before you choose your retirement location. In certain areas, it might even make sense to rent instead of own property.

4. **Taxes on social security benefits.** There are 36 states (and Washington D.C.) that do not tax social security benefits. The other states do tax to some degree, though most of these states have limits to the amount that can be taxed. Thankfully, there are a lot of ways you can avoid paying taxes on social security.

    - The degree to which this tax impacts you will depend on your other sources of income. ***If your only income is from social security, this tax will matter more to you.*** This tax will be minimal for most folks, but be sure to find out how it may impact your situation in your desired locale.

Now that you know the main taxation issues that can affect your retirement funds differently in each state, you may want to really dig into the information that's available online to make a wise choice.

Visit the Department of Revenue website for each state that interests you as a possible retirement location. The information is easy to find and available to everyone.

Everyone dreams of retiring to the perfect location, but ***some locations are more retirement friendly than others.*** If you'll do your homework before you move, it's a lot more likely that your move will be a happy one. Make an informed decision and enjoy your retirement!

Easy Ways to Cut Retirement Expenses

If you're retired, bringing in extra income isn't always an option when you find yourself in need of some extra dollars. **Depending on how well you've saved and invested for retirement, you might be looking for some ways to stretch your funds, instead.**

Fortunately, there are many easy ways to cut spending that won't significantly affect your ability to enjoy your retirement:

1. **Be flexible with your travel plans.** Consider making plans to travel in the off-season or take advantage of last-minute travel deals. Flying to an alternate airport or nearby city is another way to save money.

2. **Adjust your insurance.** Insurance needs change as your situation changes. You might find that you need less life insurance at this time. If you're driving less, you might be able to get a lower premium.

    - *Sit down with an insurance professional and assess your insurance needs.* They will almost certainly have changed with your retirement.

3. **Consider downsizing your home.** For most of us, our house is our largest expense each month. Moving to a less expensive home can make a significant difference in your monthly expenses.

    - If you also own a vacation home, think about where you'll actually spend the most time and consider the possibility of selling the other home.

4. **Try living on your retirement budget before you retire.** *A trial run of your retirement budget will give you the information you need to make the necessary adjustments.* Give yourself the chance to adjust to a new level of spending. Perfecting your budget will result in greater savings.

5. **Cut off your kids.** 60% of parents are providing financial support to non-student children. If you've been covering your kid's bills, give them fair warning that the end is near. If possible, provide a deadline and keep the money for yourself.

    - This can be challenging, but studies show that providing financial life support for your adult children commonly does more harm than good.

6. **Let go of the extra car.** With the flexibility that most retirees have, *it might make sense to only have a single vehicle.* You'll save on maintenance and insurance. If you do need two cars, perhaps one car could be considerably less expensive and very fuel-efficient.

7. **Find a less expensive locale.** There are many wonderful places to live that have lower housing costs and taxes. You can even pick a climate that you love. Keep in mind the type of recreational activities you enjoy.

8. **Find discounts.** AARP is well known for providing discounts for its members. Many businesses provide discounts for seniors.

    - Spend a few minutes each day looking through the coupons.

9. **Be aware of your entertainment expenses.** There are many hobbies and sources of recreation that are free or have a minimal cost. If a hobby is going to require expensive equipment, acquire what you need before retirement.

10. **Cut back on food expenses.** Take advantage of the early bird special or eat in. Regularly eating out can be very expensive over time. It's a great time to try new recipes and find new enjoyment in eating at home.

Ideally, retirement is an enjoyable time filled with fun, adventure, and relaxation. One way to maximize your enjoyment is to eliminate financial concerns. ***Cutting your unnecessary expenses is a great way to shore up your finances.*** Spend your money on the creation of memories.

Estate Planning Strategies

Beware of These Top 7 Estate Planning Mistakes

Most people view estate planning in the same way they view a root canal: ***Put it off until the pain is too great to ignore any longer.*** Also, those with little income or net worth believe that estate planning doesn't apply to their situation. But estate planning is much more than just the allocation of cash, real estate, and other assets. There are other things to consider, too.

There are many errors that occur again and again in estate planning. Avoiding these mistakes is half the battle.

Steer clear of these mistakes for a successful estate plan:

1. **Procrastination.** Estate planning is a little like completing a tax return. No one really wants to do it. But it's so important to push your reticence aside and get it done!

2. **Not paying attention to the conflicts that exist within your beneficiaries and estate plan.** For example, if your will declares that your husband receive your retirement account, but your ex-husband's name is still listed as the beneficiary, this could prove to be a big challenge.

3. **Not using the unified credit to your advantage.** This only applies to those with a significant net worth, but this mistake is made regularly. In most cases, assets pass to the surviving spouse. Up to $12,920,000 can be excluded from taxation.

   - If this isn't handled properly, though, the surviving spouse will only have their exclusion available when passing assets on to their heirs.

   - There are ways to potentially shelter this money from taxation in the future. ***One solution is a credit shelter trust.***

4. **Not having adequate life insurance.** Life insurance can be a great estate-planning tool for the affluent, but life insurance is vital to those with low income as well.

   - ***Consider how your family will survive financially if you or your spouse were to die unexpectedly.***

   - If you have significant wealth, you might consider using life insurance in conjunction with an irrevocable trust for tax purposes. An attorney that specializes in estate planning can make recommendations based on your unique situation and explain the details.

5. **Creating a plan that lacks flexibility.** Creating a plan with a little wiggle room will allow your heirs to take advantage of any new laws as well as use the assets in the most advantageous fashion.

6. **Not gifting assets.** In 2023, up to $17,000 can be gifted to each beneficiary per year without incurring a gift tax. This can be a great way of reducing the taxes imposed on your estate at the time of your death. You also have the chance to see how well your beneficiaries can manage your assets.

    - Additionally, you have the advantage of being able to witness someone enjoying your assets. You can't do that after you're gone!

Estate planning isn't the most enjoyable activity, but it is likely to be one of the most important things you do for your family.

Everyone should have a basic estate plan that spells out their wishes. This is important even if there are no children or assets. An attorney can be invaluable unless your estate is very simple. And even then, the $100+ it will cost to have an attorney take a look at your documents will be money well spent.

Give Living Inheritances to Your Kids with Tax-Free Techniques

Have you thought about the timing and tax issues of when your children will receive their inheritance from you?

Financial experts are saying that due to steadily rising life expectancies, many of us will live into our 80s and 90s, and your kids are likely to be in their 60s or 70s before receiving their inheritances.

Would you like to pass along some assets before they reach this age?

Fortunately, you don't have to die to be able to give them portions of their inheritance.

Consider these suggestions for some tax-advantaged strategies for passing along assets while you're alive:

1.   Talk with your children about starting education savings for each of their kids. Many states offer savings plans that grow tax-free. Some of these plans even allow kids to use their education dollars at a university in another state.

•   The sooner in your grandkids' lives you set up the education accounts, the more money those accounts will accumulate because they'll have a longer period of growth.

•   In the event you wish to give the money directly to a university, you don't have to pay a single bit of taxes to do it.

2.   Give your kids "gift" dollars each year. Whether it's for their birthdays, Christmas, or May Day, you can give each of your children up to $14,000 yearly (as of 2013) tax-free. In fact, you can give up to that amount to as many people (related or not) as you like without you or them being taxed on that money.

•   Consider how your children in their 30s could use the money when they're working so hard to raise young families.

•   Can you imagine the joy, pleasure, and perhaps stress-relief you can give to each of your kids by making some generous gifts now, without anyone paying any taxes on the gifts?

3.   Pay for expected medical costs. If you have children or grand-children that will always need a special type of medical care, give some money to the medical facility. This way, you'll avoid having to pay any taxes on the money you give, no matter how large the amount.

4.   Use your life insurance cash value. You can borrow money, tax-free, against your life insurance cash value and give it to your children. The government doesn't tax those borrowed funds, regardless of the amount you take out of your policy.

•   Your kids will also receive the funds tax-free as long as each gift is below the IRS limits ($17,000 in 2023).

•   As long as your policy stays in force, those funds remain tax-free to you. You don't need to ever pay them back if you don't want to. Upon your death, your heirs don't have to pay those dollars back to the life insurance company, either. The policy will cover the loans.

•   Keep in mind, though, that the loans will reduce the death benefit to your beneficiaries. So taking out the loans is giving your children some funds now instead of later.

When you give now to your heirs, you'll also reduce your overall assets that may be taxed upon your death.

Everybody wins:

•   You get to see the looks on their faces when you gift a large amount of money.
•   Your heirs get to use the money now, when they might really need it.
•   Your heirs will pay fewer taxes and retain more of the assets upon your death.

Surprise your children by gifting some of their inheritance tax-free now, when you can all enjoy the special time together!

Top Reasons to Revise Your Will

Perhaps you, like many others, believe that once your will has been drawn up, that's the end of the process. While wills have never been anyone's idea of fun, it's important to review your will on a regular basis. There are many reasons to pull out your will and give it a thorough review.

Let's examine the most common reasons:

1. New family members. In general, if a will is worded properly, any children that are born after the will has been signed will be entitled to the same share of the estate as the pre-existing children. Even so, if you have a new child, check with your attorney just to be sure everything is worded according to your wishes.

- Also consider how your wishes might change based on other new people in your life. What if you re-connect with a family member? What if you make a new best friend? Maybe one of them would be the person to take good care of your boat when you're gone. Consider all new people who've entered your life since you signed your will.

2. Moving. States have different laws regarding estate taxes and how property is treated. So if you move from one state to another, there may be some major issues that need to be examined. Consult your attorney anytime you move to a new state as this can have significant ramifications.

3. A windfall. A large increase in your wealth may require another look at your will. Again, this depends on your state. Some states have monetary limits for certain types of inheritance items. Creating a trust might be the right move for you now.

- With your new wealth, you may also have a greater degree of flexibility to take advantage of certain tax shelters. And you might be considering being more generous regarding who's included in your will.

4. Divorce. Most of us aren't interested in leaving anything to our ex-spouses. If you've gotten divorced since your will was drawn up, it's time to talk to your attorney. A proper and thorough revision will reduce the likelihood of the will being contested. Consider the fact that if you don't change this document, your ex could end up with everything!

5. Death. If your spouse or only child passes away, your will should undergo a thorough review. This event may radically change how you wish to distribute your assets. Back-up recipients are usually specified within a will, but it never hurts to take another look.

6.   Change of heart. Most wills are drafted by people who are still quite young. As you age, however, your wishes may change. Maybe you were very close to your brother at one point, but haven't spoken to him in the last five years.

•   Additionally, as some people age, they become more involved with charitable organizations. Maybe you'll have the desire to include such a group in your will.

Your will we most likely not be a static document throughout your life. As your circumstances, family, and social connections change, some modifications will likely need to be made.

Review the list above and note if any of these items have occurred since your will was completed. If so, schedule some time with your attorney today. In this case, more than in many others, it's better to be safe than sorry.

Insurance Strategies

Renter's Insurance and Retirees

Does your house feel empty and oversized now that your kids have homes of their own? Maybe now is the time to move to a condo or apartment. You'd be free of mowing the grass, cleaning out of the gutters, and shoveling the driveway. And perhaps best of all: no more property taxes!

If you decide to downsize your residence and rent instead of own, you'll no longer need homeowner's insurance. Even so, **you'll still have stuff to insure, and renter's insurance is your financial solution.**

What Does Renter's Insurance Cover?

Consider these attributes of coverage with renter's insurance:

1. **Loss of property.** Renter's insurance will cover the loss of your personal possessions in the same situations that your homeowner's policy covered. This will include occurrences such as fire, theft, storm damage, and water damage.

    - *Be aware that certain types of property like jewelry, high-end electronics, and antiques may require specific coverage with a rider.*

2. **Add a rider for earthquakes, floods, or hurricanes.** As with homeowner's policies, damage from earthquake and flood typically are not covered. Separate coverage or a rider is required if these are relevant to your geographical area.

    - Inquire about damage from hurricanes if those can be an issue where you live. After a hurricane, you may find it difficult to collect, so ensure you know what you're getting up front.

3. **Actual replacement cost vs. cash value.** When looking at policies, understand whether the policy covers the replacement cost or the cash value.

    - If only the cash value is covered, for example, you won't receive enough to fund the replacement of your 10-year old leather couch.

    - Purchasing a policy that provides the actual replacement cost will cover what it really costs you to replace your property, but the premiums will be higher.

4. **Policy limits.** Know the limits on the coverage within your policy. Some policies have a cap on the total payout, too.

5. **Liability.** Renter's policies usually cover some liability.

- For example, if someone slips in your apartment and breaks his arm, you're likely to be covered.

- You may also be covered if your dog bites someone, but certain breeds are frequently excluded, so be sure to check on these restrictions if you have a dog.

- Any accidental damage you cause to the building is also usually covered. So if you trip and put your shoulder through the dry wall, your insurance should cover the cost to repair the wall.

Cost

The cost of coverage is usually quite low - often no more than $100 per year.

The factors that determine the cost include the amount of the deductible, your location, and your specific needs beyond the basics. Discounts are usually available for having safety features like burglar alarms, smoke detectors, and fire extinguishers. Having additional policies with the same insurance company can also reduce your cost.

You can lower your premiums by having a sprinkler system for fire, dead-bolt locks, only non-smokers in the household, electronic payments, and a good credit rating. Electronic payments require less labor to process, so many companies charge more if you mail yours. The other items are risk management issues. A non-smoking household is much less likely to have a fire.

Before you sign up for a specific policy, ***sit down with your insurance agent and see what other premium discounts might apply to your situation.*** You could save yourself a bunch of cash.

Document Your Property

Make a list of all your belongings, with photos, before you get your policy. It would be an even better idea to make a video. Store your list or video in a private location online or in a safe deposit box at your bank. Keeping the video in the video camera won't help you much if the camera gets stolen or destroyed in a fire. The same goes for a list on your computer.

Becoming a renter instead of a homeowner doesn't mean you no longer need insurance. Your possessions still need to be insured and you still have potential liabilities. Because of this, renter's insurance makes sense. It brings you a lot of peace of mind for only a little

6 Unusual Insurance Policies You Might Want to Consider

Insurance can be a tough pill to swallow. You pay a significant amount of money and rarely get anything back in return. **Only when tragedy strikes do you make a profit.** The rest of the time, it simply seems like a money pit.

However, when you need it, insurance can save your financial life.

Certain types of insurance are a necessity. There are many types of insurance you might not consider or perhaps even know about. These unusual policies can be critical in particular situations.

These types of insurance are worth considering:

1. **Business life insurance.** If you own a business, business life insurance can protect you if one of your partners or a key employee dies. It can provide the funds needed to buy out that partner's share of the business or find a replacement. If your business is highly dependent on a super-star salesperson or inventor, this policy could save your business.

2. **Long-term care insurance.** Long-term care insurance can help to cover the expenses of long-term in-home care, as well as nursing home expenses.

    - When purchasing a policy, keep in mind that less than 10% of those that actually use it need it for more than three years. It's probably unnecessary to get a policy that will pay for significantly more time.

3. **Antique insurance.** Homeowner's and renter's insurance typically won't cover the replacement or restoration expense of antiques. This insurance will do exactly that. But be sure to check with your regular insurance policy first. In some cases, regular homeowner's / renter's policies are sufficient.

    - Think about the replacement value of your antiques. Is a policy to replace or to restore them worth it to you? If you're a collector, the answer is probably "yes." If you merely inherited one old lamp from your aunt, the answer might be different.

4. **Pet insurance.** While the cost of an operation for a pet is significantly less than for a person, it can still be very expensive. Many employers are even beginning to offer this insurance. If your pet needs significant medical treatment, this policy can be a wonderful benefit.

    - Ask yourself what you would do if your 8-year old dog needed a $5,000 operation. Do you own a breed of dog or cat that is known to have frequent health issues?

5. **Longevity insurance.** Very few people have heard of longevity insurance. It's very interesting. This insurance policy begins paying you a monthly sum after you hit a certain age. This type of insurance is quite inexpensive because many policyholders don't live long enough to receive a payout.

    - ***But if it seems like that you will live longer than average, it can be a great way ensure an adequate income during your later years.*** How long do members of your family live? How is your health?

6. **Wedding insurance.** The average wedding now costs around $25,000! Bad weather, a death, or illness can put your wedding plans on the skids. This insurance will help to cover the lost costs. The policies are relatively inexpensive. It's important to determine what will and won't be covered.

    - Also, be sure to discuss with your caterer, photographer, wedding planner, and others what happens if the wedding has to be cancelled or postponed. The answers will have an impact on your decision process.

No one enjoys purchasing insurance, but it can be a real lifesaver when unexpected tragedy strikes. **While we all hope that we'll never need it, sooner or later, many of us do.** Consider what would happen if you needed a certain policy, but didn't have it. That may be the best way to determine which policies are worth having and which are not.

Could You Benefit from Umbrella Liability Insurance?

If you prefer to plan ahead for anything unsavory that might happen to you financially, you might want to consider purchasing umbrella liability insurance. Umbrella liability insurance can protect your assets from large claims or lawsuits.

Review these elements of an umbrella liability insurance policy. Maybe the time is right for you to obtain an "umbrella" of your own.

1. **An umbrella policy is additional insurance.** You can purchase an umbrella liability insurance policy as an adjunct to your homeowners' or auto insurance policy. With some policies, you can also add to other coverage, like your boat insurance, with an additional charge.

2. **It provides extra financial protection.** Should you ever be sued for liability, having an umbrella policy to fall back on will provide extra coverage past the limits of your homeowners' or car insurance policy. For example, if you cause an accident, liability claims could easily go way past your normal policy limits for property damage or medical care.

3. **Umbrella policies are large.** *The least liability amount you can obtain through an umbrella liability policy is $1 million.* Also, most umbrella liability policies require that your main policy (vehicle or homeowner's insurance) already cover you for at least $300,000.

4. **Your assets don't have to be large.** It's not necessary for you to have $1 million worth of assets in order to obtain such coverage – or to be sued for such an amount. After all, you could, for example, get sued for a million dollars and only have assets totaling $200,000. Without an umbrella policy, your *future* income and assets are also at risk!

5. **Your family and pets are covered.** An umbrella policy covers everyone in your family living in your household, including your pets. So even if your pets get loose and cause some damage, you're covered. Many policies even extend coverage to others, such as when you let someone else drive your car somewhere and they get in an accident.

6. **Your legal fees are covered by an umbrella liability policy.** Umbrella liability coverage will even pay for your legal fees if a liability suit is brought against you.

7. **The cost for umbrella insurance is reasonable.** The first $1 million of coverage costs as little as $200-$400 per year. Each additional $1 million is only about $100. *Raising your regular deductible might even provide enough savings to pay for an extra million dollars of coverage!*

8. **Obtain an umbrella policy from your current insurer.** Ask your auto or home insurance agent about adding an umbrella liability policy to your coverage. You might even get discounts on all your liability policies when you bundle all of them with the same carrier.

Here's an example of how your umbrella liability policy would work:

You're on a car trip and have typical vehicle property liability coverage of $50,000. You're involved in a major car accident. You collide with an expensive recreational vehicle (RV). The RV is less than a year old. The insurance estimate to repair the RV is $90,000.

Your regular car insurance policy would cover only $50,000 toward repairing the RV's damage. However, with an umbrella liability policy, the remaining $40,000 worth of damage would also be paid. You won't have to pay anything out of pocket (other than your primary car insurance deductible amount).

It's a comforting feeling to know that you can protect all your current and future assets, plus cover legal fees, with such a small investment. In the unfortunate event that someone brings a liability suit against you, you'll be prepared.

Open your "umbrella" policy to protect you and your family!

Don't Let Insurance Fraud Devastate Your Financial Plans

You're probably familiar with the concept of insurance fraud, since it has been around for a long time. **The earliest recorded instance involves a merchant intentionally sinking his ship in 300 B.C.!** The merchant drowned in the process.

You might be surprised at the negative effects insurance fraud can have on your financial future and that of your loved ones. This type of fraud affects policyholders, insurance companies, and investors.

It's not always easy to protect yourself from insurance fraud. **This guide explains some of the most common fraud scenarios** so you can beware of anything that looks suspicious in your insurance dealings.

While fraud exists in every type of insurance, this discussion is about life insurance.

Insurance fraud exists in two basic forms: buyer fraud and seller fraud.

Buyer Fraud

1. **False medical information.** This occurs when the insured give false information about pre-existing medical conditions or health habits, like smoking, for example. The applicant is then able to obtain a policy with lower premiums or obtain a policy that might have been denied otherwise.

    - If the insured dies, *their family might be denied the proceeds of the policy.*

2. **Post-dated policy.** This is much more difficult to successfully pull-off now and usually requires the knowledge and assistance of an insurance agent. A policy is issued after a person's death but is made to appear to have been issued before that death.

    - Paying fraudulent claims hurts the insurance company and their investors.

3. **Lack of insurable interest.** This occurs when someone insures another person that they have no business insuring, like if you insured your neighbor, for example. *Insurance exists to protect someone from financial loss.* If you wouldn't suffer a financial loss from someone's death, you can't insure them to your eventual benefit.

4. **Suicide.** It's against the law to obtain a life insurance policy with the intention of committing suicide. It's also against the law to commit suicide with the intention of making it look like an accident so an insurance policy can be collected upon.

    - While many policies do pay in the event of suicide, it's only after a specified period of time has passed since the policy was issued.

5. **Faking Death.** This is largely self-explanatory. The insured fakes his death so the insurance payout can be collected and enjoyed by loved ones or the insured. It's difficult to hide these days, but some still attempt this type of fraud.

Seller Fraud

1. **Fake companies.** In this type of fraud, a company portrays itself as an insurance company. It issues policies and collects premiums, but never intends to pay on any insurance claims. They simply pocket the premiums and continue doing so for as long as possible.

    - Do your research before purchasing any policy to ensure that the company is legitimate. ***Check the website of your State Board of Insurance*** to determine if the company is licensed to do insurance business in your state and the company's status in other areas, like claims complaints.

2. **Churning.** Churning can be common in any industry where commissions are at stake. An insurance agent encourages his clients to buy a policy, cancel it, and repurchase. The agent can collect greater commissions this way.

3. **Premium theft.** This is less common with the automated payment systems in use now, but can still occur. The insurance agent pockets the premium and never gives the money to the company underwriting the policy. The agent gets the premiums, and the policy is cancelled for non-payment.

    - To protect yourself from an unsavory agent like this, ***make your check payable only to the insurance company and check to see who cashes it.***

4. **Over coverage.** Here the agent encourages the client to purchase more insurance than they need. The intention is to collect larger commissions at the client's expense.

Insurance fraud has varying effects, depending on the type of fraud:

- Buyer fraud tends to affect everyone associated with the insurance company, since the costs are spread to everyone. This includes policyholders, investors, and even the company's employees.

- Seller fraud typically affects individual policyholders and their families or other beneficiaries.

Researching any insurance company or agent you do business with is always in your best interest. Be smart with insurance transactions and you can be confident that your insurance will be there to help protect you and your loved ones.

Learn Annuity Pay-out Choices to Meet Your Retirement Needs

You can't beat an annuity when it comes to setting up an effective savings plan for your retirement. An annuity can ensure you'll receive a steady stream of income in your golden years.

You're guaranteed to receive payouts from your annuity (in most cases) so you can depend on those dollars when you retire. **And more good news — you have options when it's time to receive payouts.**

You can choose from these options:

1. **Period certain payout.** This type of annuity payment guarantees you a specific amount monthly (or yearly) for a specific time period.

    - For example, perhaps you select receiving $2,000 monthly over a twenty-year period. If you die before the twenty years passes, your surviving beneficiary would continue to receive the monthly payments for the rest of the twenty years.

2. **Lifetime payout.** This type of payout continues level payments throughout your life. Insurance actuarial figures are used to determine the amount of your payments, based on your age, health, life expectancy, and the total amount you paid into the annuity.

    - This option is great for a long life – **you can't run out of money.** However, if you die shortly after starting the payments, your beneficiaries get nothing under this option.

3. **Lifetime with period certain payout.** This type of payout is a blend of the period certain payout and the lifetime payout.

    - As long as you live, you're guaranteed to receive payments. Plus, the payments are also guaranteed for however long you choose when you make the option. If you die before the period is up, your beneficiaries receive the payments for the rest of the period.

    - For example, if you choose *lifetime with a 15-year period certain payout* and you die in the tenth year, your beneficiary will receive the payments for five more years.

4. **Joint and survivor payments.** This type of payout allows you to elect to receive a lesser payment over your lifetime so that your surviving spouse can continue to get payments until their death as well. ***Married couples often select this type of payout.***

5. **Lump sum payout.** When the time comes for you to start drawing on your annuity, maybe you want your annuity dollars all at once. If that's the case, you certainly have the option.

    - However, it's important to consider the tax disadvantages of this type of payment. You'll have to pay taxes on the amount you withdraw, so you might be looking at a hefty tax bill.

    - ***The lump sum payout is not a recommended choice by financial experts.***

6. **Self-selected systematic withdrawals.** This type of annuity payout is different than the others because you decide how much you want to receive and when. Of course, the insurance company can't guarantee you'll receive lifetime payments if the amount you choose is higher than the insurance company projects that you can be paid over your lifetime.

    - ***This method is risky because even though your monthly payments may be high, the funds might also deplete before you die.***

7. **No payouts.** If you've amassed plenty of money to live on in your retirement without accessing your annuity, you don't have to take any payouts at all. What this means is that all the money in your annuity will pass to your beneficiary upon your death.

Regardless of the type of payout you select, ***double-check the beneficiary information on your annuity documents*** to ensure the correct beneficiary is named along with their up-to-date contact information.

So you have plenty of choices when it comes time to start receiving payouts from your annuity. Assess your needs carefully before you choose an option so that your annuity will serve you well.

Real Estate Owner Ship

Relying on Home Equity for Retirement Could Spell Disaster

For many people nearing retirement, their home is likely to be their single most valuable asset. However, it's questionable whether or not home equity should be used to fund your retirement.

It's common to use home equity loans and reverse mortgages to access home equity to pay for retirement expenses. ***As many as 50% of those over the age of 50 report they are planning on using home equity funds for retirement.*** This number is much higher than it's been in the past.

However, there may be more risks than you've previously realized.

Consider these risks regarding home equity and retirement:

1. **Most investments have lost value.** The housing market is still struggling to recover and home equity levels have dropped in recent years in most markets. Other investments have not done well either.

    - It's likely the decreased value in other investments is driving homeowners to rely on home equity. Your home equity might be less than you think.

    - Plan for the worst and hope for the best. What if your home equity was half of what you expected at retirement? Could you successfully navigate that challenge? What can you do now 'just in case?'

2. **You always need a place to live.** The more financing you have against your home, the greater the risk of losing it should something go awry. ***Reverse mortgages and home equity loans deplete home equity.***

    - If you decide or are forced to move, you might not have enough equity left to purchase that smaller home or condo.

    - Many forms of home equity lending have higher fees and expenses than you may realize. Be certain you understand just how much that money is costing you.

    - The conversion of one asset to another is almost always associated with a cost. Ensure that cost is accounted for and understood.

3. **Economic conditions can change.** The economic climate now is lukewarm, at best. But in time, that will change. It's likely that home equity levels and investments in general will get better.

    - ***Keep in mind you can't predict what the economic conditions will be when you retire.*** The further away your retirement date, the more risk there is in trying to predict it.

    - It's always wise to assume the worst. If inflation is high and home prices are low, how viable is it to rely on your home equity?

4. **Avoid using home equity funds toward consumable items.** If you must use your home equity, purchasing a vacation or an automobile can be a big mistake.

    - Accessing home equity funds is analogous to taking on another debt. ***Taking on a debt at a time when your income is largely fixed is never a good idea.***

5. **Financial planning is always the answer.** If you don't have sound financial planning in place, it's never too soon (or too late) to start.

    - Good planning can prevent ever having to use home equity funds for retirement.
    - Put a plan in place that makes sense for your income and timeframe and stick to it.

While many plan on dipping into their home equity for retirement, it might not be the best solution. It can be a viable source of funds, but its presence can't be reliably predicted.

There are many factors that can make the value of your equity decrease between now and your retirement.

Make a good financial plan and stick to it. The ideal situation would be one in which you don't have to rely on home equity at all.

Renter's Insurance and Retirees

Does your house feel empty and oversized now that your kids have homes of their own? Maybe now is the time to move to a condo or apartment. You'd be free of mowing the grass, cleaning out of the gutters, and shoveling the driveway. And perhaps best of all: no more property taxes!

If you decide to downsize your residence and rent instead of own, you'll no longer need homeowner's insurance. Even so, ***you'll still have stuff to insure, and renter's insurance is your financial solution.***

What Does Renter's Insurance Cover?

Consider these attributes of coverage with renter's insurance:

6. **Loss of property.** Renter's insurance will cover the loss of your personal possessions in the same situations that your homeowner's policy covered. This will include occurrences such as fire, theft, storm damage, and water damage.

   - ***Be aware that certain types of property like jewelry, high-end electronics, and antiques may require specific coverage with a rider.***

7. **Add a rider for earthquakes, floods, or hurricanes.** As with homeowner's policies, damage from earthquake and flood typically are not covered. Separate coverage or a rider is required if these are relevant to your geographical area.

   - Inquire about damage from hurricanes if those can be an issue where you live. After a hurricane, you may find it difficult to collect, so ensure you know what you're getting up front.

8. **Actual replacement cost vs. cash value.** When looking at policies, understand whether the policy covers the replacement cost or the cash value.

   - If only the cash value is covered, for example, you won't receive enough to fund the replacement of your 10-year old leather couch.

   - Purchasing a policy that provides the actual replacement cost will cover what it really costs you to replace your property, but the premiums will be higher.

9. **Policy limits.** Know the limits on the coverage within your policy. Some policies have a cap on the total payout, too.

10. **Liability.** Renter's policies usually cover some liability.

    - For example, if someone slips in your apartment and breaks his arm, you're likely to be covered.

    - You may also be covered if your dog bites someone, but certain breeds are frequently excluded, so be sure to check on these restrictions if you have a dog.

    - Any accidental damage you cause to the building is also usually covered. So if you trip and put your shoulder through the dry wall, your insurance should cover the cost to repair the wall.

Cost

The cost of coverage is usually quite low - often no more than $100 per year.

The factors that determine the cost include the amount of the deductible, your location, and your specific needs beyond the basics. Discounts are usually available for having safety features like burglar alarms, smoke detectors, and fire extinguishers. Having additional policies with the same insurance company can also reduce your cost.

You can lower your premiums by having a sprinkler system for fire, dead-bolt locks, only non-smokers in the household, electronic payments, and a good credit rating. Electronic payments require less labor to process, so many companies charge more if you mail yours. The other items are risk management issues. A non-smoking household is much less likely to have a fire.

Before you sign up for a specific policy, ***sit down with your insurance agent and see what other premium discounts might apply to your situation.*** You could save yourself a bunch of cash.

Document Your Property

Make a list of all your belongings, with photos, before you get your policy. It would be an even better idea to make a video. Store your list or video in a private location online or in a safe deposit box at your bank. Keeping the video in the video camera won't help you much if the camera gets stolen or destroyed in a fire. The same goes for a list on your computer.

Becoming a renter instead of a homeowner doesn't mean you no longer need insurance. Your possessions still need to be insured and you still have potential liabilities. Because of this, renter's insurance makes sense. It brings you a lot of peace of mind for only a little money!

Beware of These 5 Common Foreclosure Scams

Everyone that owns a home values the ability to go home at the end of a hard day and close the door on the rest of the world.

Our home is our sanctuary and a big part of the reason many of us go to work every day in the first place. Unfortunately, financial challenges can put home ownership at risk; after all, your house is usually your collateral for your mortgage.

Unfortunately, there are many companies that attempt to prey on those that are in danger of losing their home. While not all companies are disreputable, many are. Let's look at the most common scams out there.

Common Foreclosure Scams:

1. **Equity Stripping.** In this scam, a mortgage lender is well aware of your challenging financial situation and pushes you to get a larger mortgage to pay off the original mortgage. This larger mortgage has even larger monthly payments than original mortgage.

    - Of course, it's only a matter of time before you have difficulty making the payments. ***The new lender then swoops in and takes your home.*** You won't have much, if any, equity left because the new loan was large enough to swallow it all up. The equity has effectively been 'stripped.'

2. **Lender Scams.** Your lender may offer to refinance your home with an interest-only payment plan. This can be great, for a while. Your payments will be much lower at first. Eventually, however, there is likely to be a large balloon payment due.

    - Many people won't be able to make the balloon payment or be able to get another refinance to stop the new foreclosure. While this is not technically a scam, ***it usually turns a bad situation much worse.***

3. **Equity Skimming.** In this instance, a buyer will convince you to sign your property over to him in exchange for making your payments. The buyer will then rent out your property and start collecting rent. The buyer will not make your payments as promised and the lender will foreclose.

    - If you have a significant amount of equity, the buyer will flip the property to another buyer at a higher price and keep all the profits. Instead of falling for this, if you're in danger of losing your home to foreclosure, ***sell it yourself and profit from your equity.***

4. **Loan Flipping.** Here your lender will encourage you to refinance your loan, with the enticement of getting extra cash for home repairs or a vacation. Shortly after you refinance, they will hit you up with another offer to refinance.

    - The additional fees and cost associated with the loans will be significant and greater than any benefits you receive. It will be even more difficult to make your payments. ***This is simply a way for a lender to extract more money from you before they foreclose on your home.***

5. **Phony Loan Transactions.** An unscrupulous lender refinances your loan and provides documentation that gives the appearance of bringing your loan current. Sometimes, these documents actually transfer your home's title to the company for a very small payment.

It's normal to be stressed and searching for solutions when your home is at stake. Many unscrupulous people are aware that you might be desperate and agree to anything that looks like a lifeline. They can discover your situation from public records. Be aware of the common scams that are out there and look out for your best interests.

There is frequently a solution available, but the potential solutions above are unlikely to be the answer you're looking for.

5 Great Retirement Locations for the Budget-Minded

It doesn't take a genius to realize that the cheaper the retirement location, the sooner you can retire. Many people envision living in a shack in the middle of the desert when envisioning inexpensive retirement locations. But nothing could be further from the truth. There are many great places to live that probably cost significantly less than your current location.

If you're willing to move to another country, there are even more options. If you've never had the chance to travel abroad, this might be the perfect opportunity.

These 5 locations will keep you happy and busy with a comfortable lifestyle:

1. **Guam can be considered Hawaii's less expensive alternative.** Guam has many benefits for those hailing from North America. The currency is the US dollar, English is spoken, and it's a United States territory.

    - Housing costs are modest, though other items can be more expensive since nearly everything is imported. The medical care is good and your current insurance is likely accepted.

    - *If you're looking for a Hawaiian climate without a Hawaiian price tag, Guam might be the answer.*

2. **Nicaragua is among the most beautiful countries in the western hemisphere.** Nicaragua is a colorful country that seems to have it all. Beautiful beaches on both the Pacific and the Caribbean are enough of a reason for many expatriates to call Nicaragua home. *The fact that it's among the least expensive countries in the world is icing on the cake.*

    - Rent for a decent apartment is around $400/month.

    - You can get medical insurance for around $100/month.

3. **Knoxville, TN is a great location if you enjoy the outdoors and city life.** With approximately 700,000 people, Knoxville is big enough to have the amenities that many enjoy. But it's not so big to have the hassles of major metropolitan areas.

    - *Outdoor amenities abound:* Smokey Mountains, Blue Ridge Mountains, fishing, hunting, and hiking.

    - Knoxville also enjoys a thriving music scene.

    - Another advantage is that there's no state income tax.

4. **Columbus, Indiana is commonly referred to as the "Athens on the Prairie."** A smaller town of approximately 45,000 people, Columbus is known for its incredible architecture. Indianapolis is approximately 45 minutes away and offers professional sports teams, several museums, and is home to the NCAA.

    - Columbus even has its own roller-derby league! Close to state parks and forests, there's plenty to do outdoors. ***Columbus combines quirkiness and small-town charm in a very affordable package.***

5. **Buenos Aires, Argentina is one of the least expensive large cities in the world.** Argentina is famous for its medical system. The public health care system, combined with a surplus of medical staff, makes health care costs extremely low. Medical tourism is very popular.

    - The public transportation system is excellent and inexpensive. ***Buenos Aires provides a European feel without a European cost.*** A nice apartment can be found for less than $400 a month and a subway ticket is only 50 cents. Restaurants tend to be expensive, however.

    - With a population of almost 3 million, it's the second largest city in South America. If big-city living appeals to you, Buenos Aires is an excellent option.

Planning your early retirement includes finding an excellent retirement location. ***Stretching your dollars further can make all the difference in the world.*** By choosing the right spot, you'll not only be able to retire earlier, you'll also be able to enjoy your dream location with a very comfortable standard of living.

Top Reasons to Revise Your Will

Perhaps you, like many others, believe that once your will has been drawn up, that's the end of the process. While wills have never been anyone's idea of fun, it's important to review your will on a regular basis. ***There are many reasons to pull out your will and give it a thorough review.***

Let's examine the most common reasons:

1. **New family members.** In general, if a will is worded properly, any children that are born after the will has been signed will be entitled to the same share of the estate as the pre-existing children. Even so, if you have a new child, check with your attorney just to be sure everything is worded according to your wishes.

   - Also consider how your wishes might change based on other new people in your life. What if you re-connect with a family member? What if you make a new best friend? Maybe one of them would be the person to take good care of your boat when you're gone. ***Consider all new people who've entered your life since you signed your will.***

2. **Moving.** States have different laws regarding estate taxes and how property is treated. So if you move from one state to another, there may be some major issues that need to be examined. Consult your attorney anytime you move to a new state as this can have significant ramifications.

3. **A windfall.** A large increase in your wealth may require another look at your will. Again, this depends on your state. Some states have monetary limits for certain types of inheritance items. ***Creating a trust might be the right move for you now.***

   - With your new wealth, you may also have a greater degree of flexibility to take advantage of certain tax shelters. And you might be considering being more generous regarding who's included in your will.

4. **Divorce.** Most of us aren't interested in leaving anything to our ex-spouses. If you've gotten divorced since your will was drawn up, it's time to talk to your attorney. A proper and thorough revision will reduce the likelihood of the will being contested. Consider the fact that if you don't change this document, ***your ex could end up with everything!***

5. **Death**. If your spouse or only child passes away, your will should undergo a thorough review. This event may radically change how you wish to distribute your assets. Back-up recipients are usually specified within a will, but it never hurts to take another look.

6. **Change of heart.** Most wills are drafted by people who are still quite young. As you age, however, *your wishes may change.* Maybe you were very close to your brother at one point, but haven't spoken to him in the last five years.

    - Additionally, as some people age, they become more involved with charitable organizations. Maybe you'll have the desire to include such a group in your will.

Your will we most likely not be a static document throughout your life. As your circumstances, family, and social connections change, some modifications will likely need to be made.

Review the list above and note if any of these items have occurred since your will was completed. If so, schedule some time with your attorney today. In this case, more than in many others, it's better to be safe than sorry.

The Top 6 Home Improvements with the Best Return

Many home improvements are little more than money pits. Some improvements don't even appeal to many homebuyers. Over $200 billion is spent every year on home renovations, but how many of those dollars are spent in a way that truly improves the value of the home?

Many people are shocked at how little their improvements added to the sales price of their home.

Some home improvements can boost your home's resale value and the level of comfort you experience while you're still living there. Unfortunately, there are other improvements that can cost thousands of dollars and provide little to no return.

These home improvements are likely to pay off better than any other:

1. **New siding.** From an investment standpoint, fiber cement siding is the way to go. Vinyl siding can crack over time, and aluminum siding ultimately ends up with dents. Even with professional installation, this is still a cost-effective upgrade.

2. **New front door.** ***Fiberglass doors are very expensive, but a mid-range steel door looks great and can easily be painted to match your home.*** The more simple the door, the lower the cost. But steel doors are so inexpensive that you can afford to pick up something nice.

3. **Garage door replacement.** While no one gets excited about replacing their garage door, some jobs just need to be done. A mid-quality garage door will add to your curb appeal and improve the functionality and sales price of your home. Garage doors are easily painted, too.

4. **Wood deck.** Nearly everyone loves to sit out on a deck when the weather permits. It's the perfect transition between indoors and the outside. It effectively adds living space, and the material costs are quite low.

    - If you're handy with a circular saw, tape measure, and hammer or drill, you might be able to install your deck yourself.

5. **New windows.** ***Newer windows eliminate drafts, reduce radiant heat in the summer, and provide much better insulation than older style windows.*** They look great, too! While windows can be expensive, the payback is quite good. Compare costs and the amount of insulation. The utility savings can be impressive.

6. **Fresh interior paint.** Although paint is relatively inexpensive, the labor can be pricey. Fortunately, anyone can tackle this task on their own. You'll save a lot of money and your house will look great. Take your time and you can do a great job.

- Stick to neutral colors that everyone can accept. If you'll be selling soon, now isn't the time for unusual colors.

Unless you're planning on staying in your home for an extended period of time, it's important to consider how your improvements will affect the sales price of your home. Many improvements do little to increase the value of your home. However, if you'll be in your home for many years, it's completely reasonable to place a priority on the enjoyment you'll receive from the upgrade.

Being the nicest house on the block might be great for the ego, but it's hard on the pocketbook. Avoid adding features to your home that aren't appropriate for your neighborhood. If you're in a middle-class setting, remodelling projects common to luxury homes are likely to be financial disasters.

A little forethought will ensure that your home improvements make your home more attractive, liveable, and valuable. **Research the costs and expected payback of any improvements you're considering.** Remember to examine the cost of labor. Nearly any project can provide a nice return, especially if you can do the work yourself.